"*Reboot Your Life* is a wonderful guide for reconnecting with the dreams we gave up to become adults." —Ron Andrews,
Vice President, U.S. Businesses,
Head of Human Resources, Prudential

"While taking a sabbatical may sound deceptively simple, making time for oneself can be a difficult task in today's busy society. Some companies, including ours, have found however, that people thrive as both individuals and as employees when they are given a sabbatical opportunity and can set aside real time to reflect, refresh, and re-energize. *Reboot Your Life* provides valuable advice, wisdom, and tips to help readers both make their sabbatical dreams become a reality and reap as much value and benefit from their sabbatical time as possible." —Tami Graham,
Director of Global Benefits Design, Intel Corporation

"It's a tough lesson to learn: Time is more valuable than money—because all the money in the world can't buy you time. And that's the lesson to be learned in these pages—how to appreciate and make the most of that uncertain and precious commodity, the time you are given to live a fulfilled life." —Terry Savage,
Nationally syndicated *Chicago Sun-Times*
financial columnist and author of *The New Savage Number:
How Much Money Do You Really Need to Retire?*

"In a world that has gone from 9-5 to 24/7 in a generation, our ability to lead a professionally productive yet reflective life is increasingly challenged. A time of professional disengagement offered by a sabbatical is invaluable. The chance to cultivate personal interests and family and friends free of the demands of the office and Blackberry leads to a richer life and thereby a refreshed perspective when returning to work. These four writers understand this and offer wise counsel. Take their advice and take a sabbatical." —Peter H. Darrow,
Senior Counsel, Cleary Gottlieb Steen and Hamilton

"During my 25 years at IMG, I witnessed professional athletes returning to competition after a needed break with re-honed skills and a fresh outlook. When I left IMG in 2006, I wanted to do the same but there were no roadmaps. *Reboot Your Life* walks you through how to plan your sabbatical, what to expect and how to reenter the work place. It's a fun, practical guide to exploring this life-changing experience."

—STEPHANIE TOLLESON,
Former Senior Corporate VP, IMG and
(current) Chair of the Board, Women's Sports Foundation

"Talk about discovery! *Reboot Your Life* gives the inspiration, insight, and practical tips to take a work break for a breather or a real life change."

—WONYA LUCAS,
Executive Vice President and Chief Marketing Officer,
Discovery Communications

"This gem of a book is from four authors who are role models of lives well lived. They provide a motivational, yet practical, blueprint for that 're-boot' that any busy person can use and apply. A must read!"

—PHYLLIS J. CAMPBELL,
Chairman, Pacific Northwest, JP Morgan Chase

"Taking a sabbatical to grow, expand and explore is so essential to your ability to create and innovate. But most of us don't think it's possible until we retire. *Reboot Your Life* gives you a road map as well as tips and stories from those who have done it. I highly recommend it for anyone thinking about making themselves, as well as their organizations, more open to innovative and creative thinking."

—CLAUDIA B KOTCHKA,
Former Vice President, Design, Strategy and Innovation
Procter & Gamble

"I don't care how good you are at your work. All of us need time off to refresh and recharge. Until recently I had never taken more than one contiguous week off from work. I wish I had taken a Reboot Break earlier in my career. *Reboot Your Life* gives you the courage and the tools to do so." —GREG JOSEFOWICZ, Former CEO, Borders, Inc.

"We all need time off from our careers to prepare for the next phase of our lives. Whether it is to regroup when we are "burned out," take care of our families when they need us most, or to explore new passions and opportunities, taking a sabbatical allows us the journey. *Reboot Your Life* is the roadmap!" —SUSAN C. KEATING,
President & CEO, National Foundation for
Credit Counseling & former President & CEO
of Allfirst Financial

"Peter Drucker, the father of management, often encouraged readers to take the time to examine their accomplishments and objectives. In his seminal Harvard Business Review article, 'Managing Oneself,' he wrote, 'To stay mentally alert and engaged during a 50-year working life, one must know how and when to change the work one does.' *Reboot Your Life* makes for a friendly, thought-provoking companion along the way." —ELIZABETH HAAS EDERSHEIM,
Author of *The Definitive Drucker* and Founder
and Director, New York Consulting Partners

"The shocks of the last decade are reminders that there is more to life than livelihoods. In this new world, the more diverse our experiences and knowledge, the more connections our brains and hearts can make. *Reboot Your Life* is a practical, relevant, inspiring easy-to-read guide on the journey for growth, rest, and renewal. The Sabbatical Sisters retreats are also an enjoyable and actionable way to give yourself the "gift of time." —SUSAN SCHIFFER STAUTBERG,
President of PartnerCom and Co-Founder
of Women Corporate Directors (WCD)

"Taking a sabbatical was one of the best things I ever did for my life! *Reboot Your Life* covers every aspect of that adventure—the fears, the money, the big dreams, other people and everything else in between. Get the book." —ARIANE DE BONVOISIN,
Author of *The First 30 Days: Your Guide to
Making Any Change Easier*

Teri —
This is about the value of taking time off!
Cathy W.

Reboot Your Life

ENERGIZE YOUR CAREER AND LIFE BY TAKING A BREAK

| THE SABBATICAL SISTERS |

Catherine Allen

Nancy Bearg

Rita Foley

Jaye Smith

BEAUFORT
BOOKS

Library of Congress Cataloging-in-Publication Data

Reboot your life : energize your career and life by taking a break / The Sabbatical Sisters, Catherine Allen . . . [et al.].
   p. cm.
  Includes index.
  ISBN 978-0-8253-0564-1 (alk. paper)
  1. Leave of absence. 2. Sabbatical leave. 3. Quality of work life. I. Allen, Catherine A.
  HD5255.R43 2011
  650.1—dc22

2010050686

For inquiries about volume orders, please contact:

Beaufort Books
27 West 20th Street, Suite 1102
New York, NY 10011
sales@beaufortbooks.com

Published in the United States by Beaufort Books
www.beaufortbooks.com

Distributed by Midpoint Trade Books
www.midpointtrade.com

Printed in the United States of America

We dedicate this book to our families.

| CONTENTS |

| INTRODUCTION |

"I always knew that one day
  I would take this road, but yesterday
  I did not know today
  would be the day."

—Nagarjuna

TIME OFF. TAKING A BREAK. Going on sabbatical. Being between gigs. These phrases describe a growing need among some of us to step out of the working world for a while. That need may be motivated by a desire to reset the balance in our lives, follow a creative dream, make a difference, give back to society, or explore something different. It may also be driven by less positive causes—job burnout, disillusionment with a career, or a life-changing event like death, illness, or divorce.

Whatever the reason, millions of us are ready for change—for a "Reboot Break"—for taking several months away from our everyday work in order to refresh and renew.

Unfortunately, most of us don't know how to do it. Or we feel we can't. Or we think we need permission. Fears about not having enough money, losing the respect of colleagues, being out of the "game," or altering that self-image keep many of us from expanding our horizons.

When we had a farm economy, natural breaks provided time to renew. As recently as the 1980s, people spent more time at home than they do today—time having dinner with their families and watching television, reading, or playing board games. There was more time for relaxation, exploring, thinking.

Today we rarely have time for rest. We have lost even our short breaks. Technology—pagers, PCs, laptops, the Internet, cell phones, BlackBerrys, and smartphones—beckons us to be "on" 24/7. Even when we're supposedly "off"—on weekends or in the evenings—we are "on," and it is taking a toll.

We're a nation on the verge of burnout. We need to take a break. We need to regroup, renew, and reinvigorate our lives. We need to give ourselves the "gift of time."

According to a 2009 Gallup Poll and statistics from Monster.com, the numbers underscore the stress people are feeling in the workplace and the desire for change. American workers are working more hours than they did twenty years ago, with men averaging 49.9 hours and women 44 hours per week. Eighty-six percent of workers are experiencing job stress, and half describe their stress as "extreme fatigue" or "feeling out of control." Sixty percent of workers feel pressure to work too much, and 83 percent of employees want more time with their families. Over 50 percent of employees are either somewhat or completely dissatisfied with their jobs, and 83 percent of workers plan to look for a new job when the economy improves.

What a testament to the need for taking time off!

To be competitive as a nation and thrive as individuals in the twenty-first century, we all need time to refresh and recharge. To be creative and productive, we must be nourished, too.

It is time to give ourselves a break and "reboot our lives."

Most would agree that Americans don't know how to take a real break, and many of us long to modify work to recapture our evenings, Saturdays and Sundays, and our vacations. Those who have taken sabbaticals have found that when they return to work, they are far more likely to take breaks in the future. They are able to acknowledge that they need them. They've seen the benefits of time that is truly "off" and the importance of pacing themselves. As one engineer told us after a six-month break, "A sabbatical actually resets our 'beingness,' making us aware of the need to check in with our inner selves."

This book is about regaining that time and creating a more desirable cycle of work, relaxation, and personal growth, and about the self-discovery and acceptance that comes from exploration and rest.

We've talked to more than two hundred people who have taken a Reboot Break—men and women from their twenties to their seventies, from a variety of ethnic, socio-economic, and professional backgrounds—to learn why they decided to take time off from work, how they did it, and what they learned.

This includes, of course, those who have had to take unexpected sabbaticals because they were laid off in a down economy. Rather than taking the first job they're offered, many people spend three to six months or more stepping back and reassessing their goals and their opportunities.

Taking time out from work to reboot your life is not just a new and enduring trend; it's a necessity in our stress-ridden world. This book will give you the guidance and resources to negotiate a Reboot Break, whatever your age and stage of life and even in tough economic times. Meaningful time off can be an important path, not only to personal development, but also to career advancement. What's more, you deserve it!

In addition to interviewing sabbatical takers about their experiences, we wanted to understand how employers are viewing sabbaticals. To that end, we have examined more than fifty corporations, law firms, non-profits, small businesses, and educational institutions that provide funding for sabbaticals, allow their employees to take unpaid leave, or support the concept in some other way. Many organizations see sabbaticals as a recruitment and retention tool that helps create a resilient and loyal workforce. Later in the book, we help you make the case to your employer for your Reboot Break and for instituting a Reboot Break policy.

SOME COMMON THEMES

One of the key themes that emerged in our interviews with men and women who took time off was the importance of planning. We spend two chapters on this (Chapters 3 and 4), one of which is entirely devoted to financial planning and the consideration of things like health insurance and retirement savings.

A second major theme was that there are at least four phases to a sabbatical:

I. Creating Space—Putting your life in order
II. Reconnection—Revitalizing connections to people, places, activities, and self
III. Exploration—Learning new things, especially through travel
IV. Reentry—Starting a new chapter of your life

We devote three chapters to these phases, Chapters 5, 6, and 7.

A third major theme was that all the people we interviewed, no matter the experience, felt that their lives had improved after the sabbatical. They experienced better career opportunities, or enhanced personal relationships, or a new sense of self-respect. We use their stories throughout the book to illustrate this.

Our mission is to empower overworked Americans and others to plan for and take much-needed career intermissions in order to rest, recharge, stimulate new thinking, and come back better prepared for the challenges and opportunities they face.

We hope to broaden your horizons by encouraging you to give yourself the "gift of time" to find your real interests and explore them. In the pages ahead, we address common hesitations and fears head-on and provide practical, easy-to-read, and actionable ways to plan, prepare for, and actualize the life-changing break from work that we call rebooting your life. Each chapter has exercises that will help you with your plan, and the Appendix is rich in worksheets and resources.

The book is designed to allow you to skip around, find topics and exercises of interest, and take what is relevant to you now. It is also designed to take you step by step through the planning and implementation of time off from work . . . what we call the Reboot Break. We hold retreats across the United States to help people think about, and plan for, their time off. The Appendix has more information about the Reboot Your Life Retreats.

We invite you to use this book as your companion, friend, advisor, and support group, all rolled into one. Our message to you is simple: *By taking time out to reboot, personally and professionally, you too can live the better, richer, fuller life you've been seeking.*

CHAPTER 1

Giving Yourself the Gift of Time

"Whatever you can do, or dream you can, begin it.
Boldness has genius, power, and magic in it.
Begin it now."

—Johann Wolfgang von Goethe

W hat would you do if you only had one year to live?" That's the question Jaye asked Nancy, Cathy, and Rita the first time we talked. It was 2006, and we were seated around a table on a veranda in Vieques, Puerto Rico. We were at the annual conference of a group of women CEOs and senior business and public policy executives who network, support each other, and give back to the community—as well as have fun. One of the ways we get to know each other better is through "table topics" at lunch.

We four had chosen the table with the topic "Dreamweaving: Following Your Dreams." Each of us wondered as we sat there awkwardly how much we would reveal of our dreams and ourselves. Who were these other women? None of us thought of ourselves as "touchy feely" or "new age," so we didn't know what to expect of the others.

It turned out we were all contemplating a sabbatical or integrating the benefits of one we'd taken. We began to realize that our dreams had everything to do with taking time off to discover what they really were or to make them happen. If we had a year to live, we each agreed, it might just be a sabbatical year.

At the end of the lunch, we agreed to check back during the year to see where we were in achieving our sabbatical dreams. "I left feeling I had a support network that would cheer me on," said Rita. "It was an unexpected result of the lunch and taught me again about how small risks are ways to open the mind and heart."

The four of us stayed in touch after the conference but did not see each other again until a few months later at a crowded New York City event. Cathy called across the room to Rita, "Hey, Sabbatical Sister, I'm going to do it—I'm going to take my sabbatical!" Rita, with a huge smile, called back, "Hey Sabbatical Sister, I just started mine!" The name Sabbatical Sisters stuck.

The book was born the next year at our conference in Ecuador, and we went on to coin the term Reboot Break as an updated term for sabbatical.

WHO TAKES REBOOT BREAKS

If you bought this book on your own, you must be thinking about taking time off. If someone else bought it for you, it may be to nudge you in the direction of a needed break. In any case, as you contemplate your own dream of a Reboot Break, your age may have a great deal to do with the kind of break you're looking for and the way you decide to go about it.

If You're in Your Twenties and Thirties

You, who are just starting out, have multiple reasons for taking time off. You may find you need a "course-correction" in your career or in the way you've balanced your life. You may feel you chose the wrong career and want to continue your education in order to switch to something more suited to you. You may want to start a family or spend more time with loved ones. Or you may just be bored with your job. Because you're young, you are probably less encumbered and more able to travel, explore new interests, give back to your community, or just try something new.

In your twenties and thirties there are many real and perceived barriers to taking some time off, but there are ways to get around them.

The three greatest fears at this age are:

- You can't afford it financially.
- You won't be taken seriously in your career.
- You won't be able to come back to your job or employer.

Later in the book we go into more detail on the real and perceived barriers to taking time off, how to deal with these barriers, and how to make time off a possibility by planning for it.

The chapters on planning and ways to fund a Reboot Break address the financial concerns. In our chapter on planning and what organizations are doing to create programs to attract and retain employees, you'll see how to convince your employer that it's in his or her best interest, as well as your own, to allow you to take time off.

Many people your age have "set themselves apart from the pack" by taking time to volunteer, upgrade skills or education, explore and travel, and come back refreshed.

If You're in Your Forties and Fifties

People in their forties and fifties tend to be mid-career and may need a break to recover from job burnout or stressful events in their personal lives like illness, death of a family member, or divorce. Or they may want to explore a totally new career, or take time to volunteer and give back. In this age group, the need to renew, refresh, and become more creative is often paramount.

Your key fears may be:

- If you leave, a peer may get your promotion or job.
- You have clients, employees, or partners who you think can't cope without you.
- You need the benefits for your family.
- You wonder if you step away whether you will ever find work again.

These fears and the others we talk about later in the book are all manageable. It just takes planning. There will always be peer competition in large organizations, but the stories from our interviewees show that taking the risk paid off. They came back to the same organizations refreshed and invigorated. They were often promoted. Or they were approached by other organizations because of their confidence and risk taking. **To be competitive, organizations are seeing that they need to retain the experienced and knowledgeable people in this age group.**

We have a discussion in Chapter 3 on how to take time off if you are an entrepreneur, a small organization employee, a partner in a law firm, or any other position where clients, customers, and employers may be significantly impacted. We show you how to do it. And we share the stories of those who have done it.

If You're in Your Sixties and Seventies

People in their sixties and seventies are showing interest in taking a Reboot Break as they increasingly reject traditional models of retirement. Many are starting new careers, exploring non-profit involvement, or launching their own businesses. They are spending time exploring their passions, from art to travel to grandparenting. Some are taking a "pre-retirement break" to explore what they want to do when they eventually leave work.

At this age, the fears may be more philosophical than just juggling finances and responsibilities. But there are still concerns that must be addressed:

- You are stepping off the career track. Can you get back on if you want?
- Have you saved enough for retirement, and will this impact finances and benefits negatively?
- What will you do with all that time?

Baby Boomers hate the "R" word (retire) and want to do something different, but don't know what. Taking time off at this juncture of your life gives you time to explore different options and plan for the next phase of your life. Baby Boomers are likely to live well into their eighties and nineties, and be far healthier than their parents. There is much you can do, and rebooting may help you figure out what you want to do for the next twenty to thirty years.

Why is it we often undervalue one of our most valuable assets—time? Anyone over sixty will tell you how important it is, but at twenty or thirty, we think we have all the time in the world to do what we want. We willingly spend time working and planning our finances, our careers, or our vacations, but we rarely spend time planning how to step back for a while and decide what we really want to do. People contemplating sabbaticals worry, "What will I say when people ask what I'm doing now?" or "What do I put on my business card?"

We in the United States are so tied to what we do that leaving our jobs, even temporarily, is a scary proposition.

THE GIFT OF TIME

Remember the play and movie *Stop the World—I Want to Get Off?* We have all felt that way. Our days are full of obligations, demands, and details. From the time the alarm goes off to when we collapse in bed at night, we bounce from activity to activity.

For most of us, our busy schedules are what enrich our lives. We love coaching basketball while we tap at our BlackBerrys in between plays. We like pushing ourselves at our jobs and crossing things off our lists. Being busy is a way of life, and most of us like it that way—at least until we don't.

Do you ever find yourself thinking:

Why do I do this to myself all the time?

What if I could clear my schedule for a week, a month . . . a year?

Inwardly, many of us are yearning to take some meaningful time off from work, to give ourselves the gift of time.

Think forward. Imagine a period of richness and fulfillment. Imagine floating in your own time—fast if you want, slow if you want. Imagine responding to your own internal rhythm more than to external stimuli and requirements. How would that feel?

Imagine some more: You are getting things done that you've left undone for years, trying new things, spending real time with friends, being with family, stretching yourself mentally and physically, and filling your mind with something other than cell phone messages and schedules.

Dream along with us some more. Here's the end game: You're back from your sabbatical. You are refreshed and reenergized. Your mind is clear and focused. So are your priorities. You've rebooted.

Now, flash back to where the journey begins: deciding that the benefits of a sabbatical are right for you, and then going through the essentials that will get you there.

The decision to take a sabbatical—to answer that call to oneself—is a huge step. There's no question about it. The worries that can cloud people's minds and tighten their guts as they contemplate taking a break are real and practically universal. At the same time, **sabbaticals are as old as time and are a natural rhythm of life**. Knowing that and learning a little more about sabbaticals—like their cultural context and great outcomes—may make it easier to decide to take one. So let's get more comfortable with the concept and explore how taking a sabbatical is a natural human desire and can make a big difference in one's life.

A LITTLE HISTORY

The Bible's Old Testament tells the story of the Sabbath. It teaches that God created the world in six days and rested on the seventh. The Bible tells us that the work-rest balance, the fourth of the Ten Commandments, was handed down by God to Moses and from Moses to his people. This idea is probably familiar to you, even if you're not religious. The concept of the Sabbath recognizes the universal need for a renewal break.

We just call that "rebooting."

In Biblical times, the practice that left fields fallow in the seventh year was called Shemitah. Also during Shemitah, individual debts were forgiven, and slaves were released from bondage. Similar to a sabbatical period, Shemitah was a time of release and freedom, symbolic of returning to oneself.

Like taking a Reboot Break today, the decision to live freely was a difficult one. Some Hebrew slaves remained slaves even though they had the legal right to become free. For them, the known was more comfortable than the unknown. Perhaps they told themselves, "Seven years from now, I'll take my freedom," postponing that challenge and its potential gifts, just as many of us now say, "Someday I will take real time off from my job. Someday I'll take time for myself." Perhaps the indebted even listened to the inner voice so many of us have heard, whispering that they did not deserve the freedom.

European culture has managed to preserve a modified version of the sabbatical practice. It's not uncommon for some Europeans to get (and take) six to eight weeks of vacation each year. That's their rebooting period. Americans, on the other hand, have a worldwide reputation for their short vacations, or for taking no vacation at all. And most Americans tend to work longer hours than people in most other developed countries. So we start from a personal time deficit each year and keep building the time debt to ourselves year after year. It takes a sabbatical to step away and recharge.

American universities have been ahead of the rest of American society. They have long recognized (beginning back in 1880 with Harvard) that professors need to get away from teaching every few years to refresh and renew. Most academic institutions grant faculty members a sabbatical of several months to a year every six or seven years for research, study, or writing. The late computer science professor Randy Pausch, famed for his "last lecture" and book by the same name, took an academic sabbatical to fulfill his lifelong dream of working as an Imagineer at Disney.

THE NEW SABBATICAL (REBOOT BREAK): IT'S NOT JUST FOR ACADEMICS

The new sabbatical—what we call a Reboot Break—is based on the same historical theories of rest and renewal as the academic sabbatical, but it offers *all* working people the opportunity to refresh and come back to the working world stronger and more creative.

The Reboot Break can be done in agreement with one's workplace, or by separating from it. It may include pay and benefits, or it may not, thus requiring a plan for financing and insurance. Taking a break entails a little thinking outside the box, but not more than most people can handle when armed with information, creativity, and determination.

How long is a Reboot Break? Ideally, it is a period of at least three months. People need at least that much time to truly benefit. With more time, the reward becomes deeper, so a year is even better. Whatever its length, a sabbatical is the gift of time, and it cannot be crammed into a night or weekend or even a one- or two-week vacation.

What is the formula? The Reboot Break has no precise formula. It takes many forms, and anyone at any stage in his or her adult life can take one.

What are some of the benefits? Time is precious, and time spent with yourself is especially precious because it allows you to examine your assumptions, habits, career choices, priorities, and purpose in life. For the more than two hundred people we interviewed for this book (what we like to call "the Reboot Break chorus"), the break provided the opportunity to think and reflect in a way they could never do in the rush of their everyday lives. All interviewees said they were personally and professionally better for their Reboot Break—in their work, in relationships, mentally, and physically.

One member of our Reboot Break chorus, Kate, thirty-five, tells her story:

I now work forty to forty-five hours a week, see friends, eat dinner with my kids at least four times a week, have dates with my husband, and am happy—and very productive—in my work. I have a ton of energy, and my creativity is back.

A year or so ago, I was in a very different place. I was lucky if I ate one dinner a week with the kids. My cat couldn't even depend on eating before 10 pm if I was feeding him. The plants in my office were dying, and I hadn't had sex in six months. By the time I realized that I was too stressed even to like my job anymore—much less enjoy my life—my family already knew that I was unhappy and unfulfilled. But their disapproving looks barely registered on me.

Then my company—a maturing startup—instituted a sabbatical program and I qualified. Actually, I was sort of nudged toward it by management, and they were helpful in providing my full salary and benefits. Together we created a plan for covering my work while I was away, and it turned out to be great training for more junior members of the team.

I had fought tooth and nail for that job, and I wanted to keep it and to love it again. The sabbatical was the answer. On my four-month sabbatical, I cleared some of the clutter from my house and life, reassessed my priorities, traveled first with my family, then alone on an adventure, and worked on my relationships. When I returned to work, the company welcomed me back and—armed with my sabbatical lessons—I became a better, more focused employee who really does love her job.

* * *

REBOOTING YOUR LIFE: TWO PATHS

For most people, the first and most important questions in preparing for a Reboot Break are: Do I want to take a break from my current job and then return there? Or will I leave my position and, when the sabbatical is over, look for something new?

These are the two sabbatical paths:

- A **workplace sabbatical**, in which you leave your job for a time of renewal and then return to the same job.
- A **between-gigs sabbatical**, in which you leave your current job and take a break before moving on to a new job or different line of work.

Which may be right for you?

Of course, not everyone's time off fits neatly into one category or the other. Some people leave their jobs with every intention of going back, and then decide not to return. Some people arrange their next job before leaving their current one, scheduling the sabbatical for the months in between. Some even retire and then figure out that they want to go back to work, creating an unexpected sabbatical.

The Workplace Sabbatical—Freedom with a Safety Net

Are you ready for a break from your job, but committed to the organization and want to return to do bigger and better things there? Are you happy with your career choice and want to stay in the track you are on, but with time out for personal renewal, or more education, or an adventure? Are you a few years from retirement and want a break to explore what you'd love to do in retirement?

In all of those scenarios, it may be that a workplace sabbatical is right for you.

Each year, thousands of Americans leave their jobs temporarily for a much-deserved break of months, a year, or longer. How do they do it?

Formal Programs

Because relatively few of us work for companies with formal sabbatical policies or know someone who's taken substantial time off—and because our culture tells us that two weeks of vacation is enough—we tend to think it's impossible. **In fact, scores of organizations, from multinational corporations to tiny non-profits, offer sabbatical programs. And those that don't have official policies are making deals with their employees that allow them much-needed time to reboot their lives.**

The Families and Work Institute, a non-profit research group, surveyed 1,100 companies with fifty or more employees for its 2008 National Study of Employers and found that 24 percent of companies with fewer than one hundred workers and 14 percent of companies with one thousand or more workers allowed paid or unpaid sabbaticals of six months or more.

Intel, based in Silicon Valley, California, has had a sabbatical program for fifteen years. More than 69,000 employees have taken time off to date. Everyone in the firm is eligible after seven years, regardless of level. It is a two-month program to which employees may add four weeks vacation time, so many end up with three months off. While people are on sabbatical, their colleagues take up or redistribute their work.

Keith took two sabbaticals at Intel and benefitted greatly from both. The first gave him time to be with his family and travel. The second helped him make some decisions about the next phase of his life.

Henry, also an Intel employee, said, "It is a great break. No one checks email and even if you do, you don't have to solve the problem. It is a great way to free yourself from the responsibilities of work for reinvigoration." Both Keith and Henry feel the program keeps people coming back to Intel and broadens the skill set of the workforce. The process of delegating responsibilities and empowering others to do the job of the person on sabbatical has led to a much more diversified and effective employee group.

Intel employees are no different from the rest of us. Their jobs are demanding. Their co-workers depend on them. And Intel is the same as any company: competition is intense; it can't afford to let projects go undone.

So how does it work? It's not as hard as it sounds. First, the employee has to plan. He tells his manager of his intention to take advantage of the program. Together, they decide on the length and timing of the sabbatical. He works with management and co-workers to ensure that his job gets done while he's out. He commits to a date when he'll return.

Though sabbaticals certainly make employees happier, companies don't grant sabbaticals to be nice. They do it because sabbatical programs make good business sense. They make companies stronger. Employees come back refreshed and recharged, with new energy and creativity and gratitude to the company that gave them a sabbatical. Organizations get a periodic infusion of new blood while retaining the work experience and wisdom of their seasoned employees. And staff members who cover for those on leave have opportunities for meaningful professional growth.

Commonfund, an asset management company based in Connect-icut, has about 170 employees and a paid sabbatical program that allows for eight weeks off. The first sabbatical is given after ten years of service, and then one is given for every seven years after that. Vacation time can be added to the sabbatical time. Employees must complete forms that describe the purpose of the sabbatical, and they must create a corporate coverage plan for while they are gone.

"The employees are great at covering for each other," Alyssa Kraft, Managing Director of Human Resources, says "because they work as teams." Commonfund is instituting changes to the program to make it mandatory for all US-based employees, from secretaries to the CEO, and to require that sabbaticals be taken within thirty-six months of earning them to encourage more employees to see the benefits of time off. "All employees have come back," Alyssa says, "They found out it was a great way to rejuvenate themselves, to refresh, and to return to work with new insights and ideas."

Sabbaticals are also great recruiting and retention tools. They breed employee loyalty, which begins with the attraction of the sabbatical program and is reinforced by the sabbatical experience.

Consider Andy, a marketing manager at a mid-sized biotech company. He took a company-approved sabbatical to travel. After six months hiking the Himalayas, exploring Eastern cultures, eating exotic foods, and meeting new people, he was excited to return to work. He missed his co-workers, whom he considered friends.

When he sat down at his workstation that first day back, Andy found that he could see the problems his team faced with fresh eyes. During his first few days, he was able to break through several challenges that had stumped his teammates and his boss. When a new project landed on his desk, he found his creativity was heightened. He worked more quickly and noticed that he was enjoying the intellectual stimulation. Work didn't feel like work.

Andy's boss, Eleanor, loved his new energy and ideas. But most exciting was that Andy wasn't a new employee. He held all the valuable knowledge, work experience, and wisdom of a seasoned worker. When Eleanor commented to Andy on his improved performance, he said he thought the whole team had been improved. Eleanor agreed. While Andy was out, she had seen his co-workers take on new responsibilities, making the whole department stronger and more flexible. Now Andy could delegate more work, giving him more time to be creative and strategic.

Everyone knew that Andy had been on a company-approved sabbatical. Because they were working with someone who had actually done it, new employees who were told about the program when they were hired became more interested in it. In his review, Eric, an administrative assistant in Andy's department, told Eleanor how important it was to him to work for a company who understood people's need for time off. He said he was committed to staying with the company long enough to do what Andy did.

* * *

If There Is No Formal Program

But what if your employer doesn't offer a formal sabbatical program? You're not alone: most companies don't. The majority of people who take sabbaticals are granted them informally.

When there is no formal program, the onus is on you to convince your boss to let you go. The key is to be able to make the business case: articulate how your sabbatical will benefit the company rather than focusing on why you need time off. (For more on this, see Chapter 3, "It's All in the Planning.")

Once the time off is granted, you'll have to negotiate the details. Approach the conversation as carefully as you would the terms of a new job. Know how much time you want to take. If you would like to be paid and receive benefits while you're gone, ask for them up front. If you don't think you're getting the amount of time you need, consider taking some of the leave without pay. (Read more about this in Chapter 4, "Funding Your Freedom.")

Mary described her sabbatical in equally glowing terms. "At forty-three and just after 9/11, I was trying to juggle a high-pressure career in commodity trading with my roles as wife and mother. Twenty years in the white-hot intensity of the trading floor had exhausted me and burned me out. And I was on emotional overload. My father was dying. I knew I needed to take time off for my own good, personally and professionally."

Mary took the scary step of asking for a three-month sabbatical, knowing no one at her company had ever taken one. To ease her anxiety, she first approached the company's human resources department for advice and confirmation that what she wanted to do was possible. With their encouragement and support, she went to her manager, who immediately approved her request. She was relieved, though she had been prepared to quit if they had not granted her the time off. "Otherwise, I would have had a breakdown," she said.

She took the sabbatical without pay and had to cover her own benefits at the company rate, but her job was guaranteed when she came back. A woman came down from the office to do her work on the trading floor during her absence. Planning and preparation were important to insure that her reentry would be as smooth as possible with her clients, so she let them know by newsletter about her impending sabbatical. They were surprised, but in a positive way. Some were even jealous.

"I came back energized and better prepared to deal with the stress and pressures of the job and environment. The job used to own me, but now I'm in control of it. I'm a better performer, and I enjoy my work more." Her career stayed on track, and she was thrilled to soon be promoted to senior vice president. On the personal front, too, the sabbatical was a resounding success, as Mary learned to balance her life better. Her experience inspired her husband to take a sabbatical the following year, and together they have created a much more satisfying and fulfilling family life, individually, as parents, and as a couple.

Unlike Mary's case, it may take a bit of convincing to get your boss or co-workers to agree to let you take a sabbatical and to negotiate the details to your satisfaction. This can be a challenge, but it can be managed, as described further in the planning chapter.

The other category of sabbaticals is a bigger leap than the workplace sabbatical but no less popular and no less feasible, once you decide to do it.

THE BETWEEN-GIGS SABBATICAL: DECLARING YOUR INDEPENDENCE

When people ask Kim what she's doing these days, she just smiles and says, "I'm between gigs." People who know her know this means she's left one job and is taking time out before starting another. She loves the freedom, the excitement, and the anticipation of having unhitched herself from what for so long has defined her: her job.

You may want a between-gigs sabbatical, too. Are you ready for a job change? Maybe you are burned out where you are, or dissatisfied with your career choice? Maybe you want to go back and fulfill an old dream or explore new career ideas. Have you retired and are now restless and starting to think about an encore career? Maybe you are out of a job—not at your choosing—and need time to figure out what to do next.

Being between gigs is about untethering from a job, either to figure out what to do next or to take a break before starting a new gig. Some people leave to search for an entirely different career that will satisfy them more deeply. The sabbatical provides the luxury of time to step back, relax, reassess, and figure out where and what you really want to be or do.

A between-gigs sabbatical offers a real sense of freedom. The job has been left behind and there are new fields to find and adventures to discover. One can spend time on special personal projects and activities before turning attention to the next gig, whether it is in the same field or a whole new endeavor.

How much time, you ask?

It varies by person (and financial circumstances), but sabbatical veterans agree that it's sensible to wait at least several months or even a year before actively looking for the next gig.

If the sabbatical taker doesn't know what the next gig will be, or even what field she or he will be in, a between-gigs sabbatical can have more of an open-ended quality than a workplace sabbatical: "Carry me away. Let the tide take me where it will. Let's see how long it takes to figure out my next career step."

Beverly needed more than just a break from working. A California pediatrician, she was becoming more and more disillusioned with the healthcare system, which was preventing her and her colleagues from giving their patients the attention they needed. So she left her practice.

It was a wrenching decision that took years to make, but she finally did it.

Beverly used the time off to get a master's degree in public health. She also traveled, visited friends, and connected with her grown children. She honed her medical skills and stayed current professionally through committee work at the local children's hospital.

Today Beverly is back at work, consulting and working on committees. She's still looking for a full-time job, but she's awaiting the right opportunity that will allow her to truly make a difference in health-care policy.

Between-gigs sabbaticals also can bring surprises. Jason, as the manager of an art-framing store, was uninspired in his work, and he was willing to sacrifice income for a job that made him happy. While he was between gigs, he spent time with his brother, who was very ill. One day when he was massaging his brother's shoulders, a light bulb went off. He could be creative with his hands through massage. Not long afterward Jason enrolled in massage school.

Today, Jason makes less money as a massage therapist than he did as an art framer. But he knows his sabbatical led him to a happier and more satisfying life. "Life's too short to work every day at a job that you don't like," he said. "And you can't think about what you want to do next while you're working. Being between gigs without a set job to go to can be daunting. But it can be exhilarating, too."

THE UNEXPECTED SABBATICAL: LEARNING TO LOVE YOUR LAYOFF

Because of ups and downs in the economy and employment trends that have made it much less likely that a person will work forever (or for many years) for the same employer, many of us will experience some kind of unexpected layoff or furlough in the course of our careers.

Losing a job can be like having a life raft snatched away. Your first reaction is survival: grab another job, quick! Within a few hours of getting the news, you're dusting off your resume, making calls, looking at the want ads. The search is on, and it is overlaid with extraordinary worry about what comes next.

Thousands of good, talented people find themselves in this situation. It is one that often raises a lot of questions: Should you get more schooling or training to enhance your credentials? Should you move to a city with more job opportunities in your field? Should you use this opportunity to change fields?

The best solution might be to take a short time out. You probably have been working since you were twenty-one or younger. If you build in a few months to reassess and figure out what to do before you start looking, you may be more likely to end up in a job you find rewarding.

How you use that time-off period will affect the longer-term success of your career and life. Many employers provide outplacement services for their employees to assist them with the sudden transition, but outplacement firms we interviewed say that many of the people entering into their programs and the job market are unfocused and not ready, and therefore they don't present themselves in a confident way. They agree that many are in need of an emotional break and a time to reflect on what they really want and need to do next. Jumping at any job is not the answer. It wastes time, tarnishes your resume if it doesn't work out, and reinforces any negative feelings you might have about being unexpectedly out of work.

You also may need time to heal wounds. On a Wednesday in June, Barbara was dismissed as president of a corporate division, leaving her feeling hurt and humiliated. In shock, she moved to her country house, deciding to put off any serious job hunting until the end of January.

The beginning period was very hard. I don't know where the time went. I got up early every day and went to the gym every morning. If I got one thing done in a day, it was a lot. I was very weepy. I had lost my identity, and I went through a people-controlling stage. I was in their faces. If I couldn't control what was around me, I was going to control others. I had such anger over the loss of my job.

Then I read a book on the five steps of transition, and it led to a lot of soul searching. The key question was, "What would make you click for the next stage of your life?" I needed to move from making my mark to doing something that made me happy.

Gradually, I got my ego back. I traveled to Italy and France for two weeks to see good friends. I reworked my bio and began using the services of an outplacement company. I formulated my strategy, talked to people, assessed my opportunities, and connected with retail headhunters and women entrepreneurs. Almost a year after I lost my job, a recruiter who received my resume said that I would make a great recruiter. After a trial run in that company, I decided to take a risk and go into this totally new field.

I am comfortable in my own skin in this new place of self and work. My sabbatical was a gift. Here's my advice: Do it. Time goes by very quickly. It takes three to six months to decompress from the rat race. It then takes three months to feel normal, especially after a job loss.

Lisa was a computer programmer who had worked for the same company for seven years. Her job had become more and more stressful, and she knew the company was reorganizing and cutting costs.

Even though she had seen it coming, Lisa felt angry when her manager told her they were cutting her position. She had worked hard and liked her job. She had been a good employee. It didn't seem fair.

After a few weeks, the dark clouds that had been hanging over Lisa began to clear. For the first time in years, she stayed at home for hours at a stretch, giving much-needed attention to the fixer-upper she had bought five years before. She started to sleep more and eat healthier foods. She began to feel relaxed and more in touch with who she really was.

Lisa had always had a strong spiritual side, and she used her newfound freedom to study Buddhism with a well-known teacher. She traveled with him to Italy, Africa, and then Vietnam, deepening her practice.

Her time off let Lisa detox from the bad feelings of being laid off, explore a long-held interest, and focus on a new goal: changing careers. Today, she's left programming behind and works in corporate giving. She continues to practice Buddhism and take occasional trips with her teacher. She says she's never been happier.

If you are laid off without an economic cushion—such as a buyout or at least six months of severance pay—the economic worries stemming from job loss can be frightening. How do I pay the bills, the college tuition? Do we cancel our family vacation? How long can I go on without a salary? Chapter 4, "Funding Your Freedom," will show you ways to buy yourself a few months if you didn't receive adequate severance pay or a buyout.

Joe's company was taken over, and the new company had its own person for his job. Joe had just bought a new home, and his son was about to start college. There were more bills to pay than ever. Naturally, Joe's first impulse was to grab for that life raft.

But two months into his job search, Joe had to admit that he had no interest in finding another job in human resources. He realized he wanted something totally different.

Instead of sending out resumes, Joe shifted gears. He bought himself a few extra months by selling one of the family cars and making other adjustments. He used his time to learn how some of his skills might transfer to a different career, public relations. "I was more scared than I've ever been," Joe said. "But reinventing myself was exciting. I love my new job."

Losing a job may turn out to be a blessing in disguise, providing you with the impetus to make the changes you may not have realized you wanted to make. The key is to shift your mindset from feeling like a victim to taking charge.

Jim had found himself with unexpected time off a couple of times in a short period. Each time his instinct was to find a new job as quickly as possible. He jumped into two different jobs, one after the other, with little thought about what he really wanted. After the second job change, he stepped back and decided to pursue his long-term dream of co-owning and running a bed-and-breakfast on Cape Cod.

Finances were the biggest issue, but he was able to live on severance and accrued vacation pay while using a home equity loan to pay for the renovation of the bed-and-breakfast he bought with a friend.

Not everyone is as certain about what he wants to do as Jim, but many, forced by a sudden change in their working environments, realize that taking a step back is the only way to move forward.

In summary, leaving a job unexpectedly can be the impetus to make the changes you have always wanted to make. Shifting your mindset from a victim of circumstances to taking charge and using the unexpected time to redirect your life can also be seen as an unexpected gift. The key is to take control of your life!

IS A SABBATICAL REALLY FOR ME?

Taking a sabbatical sounds great, right? Why, then, do so many people stand at the edge of a divide between doing a sabbatical and not doing it, wondering if they should take the leap? They are so tempted as they stand there looking at the possibilities, but they are rooted to the ground in deep thought and a certain amount of turmoil. There are decisions to make and details to handle. They think it may be easier not to take the big step. They wonder if they will lose their identity while not working, and lose their edge when they return to work. Somewhat like the Hebrew slaves mentioned earlier, people today sometimes choose to continue working simply because it's easier than taking up the challenge of freedom.

Maybe this sounds like you. It was certainly us.

Some skeptical onlookers may question why someone would step out of a job, especially a job they like and value, for a few months or a year, for some loosely defined purpose, and then return.

One might ask the same of a parachutist: "Why would someone jump out of a perfectly good airplane?!" To the sport parachutist, the answer is obvious: he or she doesn't doubt that the experience is worth the leap from the security of the plane. Careful planning has preceded the jump. There is always some risk, but the exhilaration, confidence, and focused determination gained from this experience are larger and more important than the risk. In fact, without the risk, the meaningful experience sought cannot be found.

No one can tell you when the time is right to reboot your life. What we can tell you is this: **whenever you decide to do it, it will be worth it**. When you begin to live your life differently after your time off, spending more time doing what you love, you'll feel its power in your life. When you start a new career that you'd never dreamed of when you walked out of your old job, you'll know it was the greatest gift you ever gave yourself. When you return to the office brimming with energy and ideas, you will see what a difference rebooting your life can make.

The trick is to believe what the parachutist knows: it's worth the risk.

All you need is to give yourself permission to take the leap.

YOU MAY SAY, "My life doesn't need rebooting. It's fine. I'm a multi-tasker, and I enjoy my long days and the rush I get from pressure."

Yes, but ask yourself: "Am I as strategic and successful as I could be in my work? Am I as thoughtful to my family and friends as I might be? Am I too focused on one area of my life?" Taking time out to change and do new things can bring a whole new perspective on how to approach your work—and your life.

Our experience and research show that life can be better after a break to refresh, get some space, and recharge. Furthermore, in today's workplace, people who take a sabbatical have an edge. They have figured out how to balance their life and be better at what they do.

▶ EXERCISES

Exercise 1-1: Thinking It Through

Use a journal or notebook for answering these exercises and those at the end of each chapter. Try to answer quickly, almost stream-of-consciousness, to get your ideas down on paper.

- What prompted you to read this book?
- Why do you think you need to take time off? Write down what stresses, desires, or pressures are driving this decision.
- Which kind of sabbatical (workplace or between-gigs) is right for you?
- What are your fears, obstacles, and anxieties about taking time off?

CHAPTER 2

Types of Sabbaticals: The Why and What

"Don't be too timid or squeamish about your actions.
All life is an experiment.
The more experiments you make, the better."

—*Ralph Waldo Emerson*

Sabbaticals, or Reboot Breaks, typically fall into seven types:

- Career enhancement
- Course-correction or reinvention
- Family-related
- Emotional healing
- Volunteering
- Life-enhancement
- Pre-retirement

These categories are not hard and fast, though, because **behind every sabbatical decision are uniquely individual motivations, and the mixture of motivations for sabbaticals makes them hard to fit into tidy boxes. As you read, you'll probably recognize yourself in one or more of**

the types and find yourself thinking about your own situation and motivation. The idea is not to choose a type—though that may happen. The idea is to begin to understand why a sabbatical appeals to you and just how ready you are to reboot.

CAREER-ENHANCEMENT SABBATICAL

A career-enhancement sabbatical may be right for you if:

- *You need a graduate degree or special training to move ahead.*
- *You want to explore something new or a new aspect of your current specialty.*
- *You enjoy learning and want to take your knowledge to the "next level" or to learn something new and interesting.*

Nancy's first Reboot Break was for career enhancement.

I was thirty and had been working for seven years. At that point, I was on Capitol Hill, where I first worked for the Senate Armed Services Committee, then moved to the Congressional Budget Office. I needed an advanced degree to move ahead in my career, and my boss suggested that I get a master's degree from the Kennedy School of Government at Harvard. I was thrilled to be accepted and to get a student loan. I resigned from my job and left Washington DC behind temporarily. I returned to find a job at the Pentagon directing an office and working on Middle East/Persian Gulf issues. My Reboot Break was a wonderful ten months and a great career boost.

A career-enhancement sabbatical can be taken from the workplace or between gigs, to burnish credentials for the next career move, like Nancy's. The motivation may be higher pay, more job satisfaction, or a climb up the ladder to a position with greater responsibility. It can also be an excuse to take time off to come back a better, recharged employee. Inevitably, people who take these Reboot Breaks add personal experiences to their time off, such as travel or more time with the family.

Sandra is a grade school teacher in the Bronx, New York, who took a one-year educational sabbatical at age forty-seven to increase her salary and spend more time with her young son. She had been working for seventeen years in the New York school system, which allows a one-year sabbatical with partial pay after fourteen years of service.

To obtain her master's degree, Sandra took three classes each semester, concentrating the classes all on the same day so that she would have the other days free. She wanted to be at home for her fourth-grader and be his class parent. Also, her husband had some health issues, and for several months he was at home out of work. She told us, "I was so glad to be completely free to take him to the doctor and be there with him. Our family life and bonds benefited so much from this break."

Career-enhancement sabbaticals can be very satisfying, as they offer a real change of lifestyle—away from work—that encompasses more than just professional improvement. Instead of squeezing in night classes while they work during the day, people who take career-enhancement sabbaticals are able to engage fully in the academic experience.

Lauren's Reboot Break and MBA were fully paid by her corporation. She said of this time, "It was wonderful being a full-time student and being able to separate who I am from the job I do. Not having a work identity while I was in school was very empowering."

Some corporations let their up-and-coming executives spend time in Washington DC for a stint in the corporate affairs office. Others allow employees to spend time in the government, such as being a White House Fellow. John, a former executive with Bethlehem Steel, spent time in Washington DC when it was important for the steel industry to understand and influence policy in Congress. "It was one of the best experiences I had in my career, enabling me to see how policy was developed and influenced. It was valuable not only in my Bethlehem Steel career, but later when I moved into other industries."

Sometimes a break is essential to creating the space to concentrate and make the career enrichment actually happen. As people learn and explore more, they often become more insightful about what they really want to do.

COURSE-CORRECTION OR REINVENTION SABBATICAL

You may be looking for a course-correction sabbatical if:

- *You are bored with your job and dream of doing something else.*
- *You were discouraged when you were younger from following your passions and doing what you really wanted to do.*
- *You feel that you have a "calling" but you're not sure what it is.*

Cathy's first Reboot Break was a course-correction from the academic to the corporate world in the 1970s.

I had always thought being a professor would be the ideal position for me. I would teach subjects I loved to students who were attentive in a bucolic setting with like-minded people.

The reality was much different. As an assistant professor, I did like my subject (management and marketing) and my students. But the pettiness and politics of academic life came as a huge surprise. So much time was spent on things of so little importance. So little was accomplished when there were so many major issues to address. Most disappointing was the lack of resources and time for research, which was what I really wanted to do.

My first Reboot Break, which included traveling and lecturing in Asia for a year, was planned as a way to get some time and space to decide whether I wanted to stay in the academic world and consult, or take the leap to the corporate world. I had sent out my resume to several corporations before I left for the year. Dun & Bradstreet, for whom I had consulted, was one of them. When I got back, they had a position waiting for me. They told me that my confidence in taking a year off demonstrated to them that I was exactly the kind of person they wanted to head a new entrepreneurial division of the company.

Many people go to work every day with a terrible secret: they know they've chosen the wrong career, but they don't know how to get out of it.

A course-correction or reinvention sabbatical can help you explore possibilities for change and lead you in a new or even unexpected direction. In some cases, the change is returning to an old dream. Maybe you always wanted to be a painter or a writer, but your parents steered you toward law because it was more practical. Or maybe you wanted to run your own small business, or be a school teacher, or use your foreign language talents, but ended up doing something else.

Brian always loved music. He played drums in high school and in college, where he majored in music. After college, Brian discovered he had a talent for stocks. He became involved in finance and moved from Virginia to New York City. But he never forgot his dream. "I was successful, but I wasn't fulfilled," he said. "Music was calling me." So he took a Reboot Break to figure out how to bring music back into his life. Today, at twenty-nine, he is a substitute music teacher in the Virginia public schools, gives private percussion lessons, and does gigs with orchestras. The next step toward his dream of performing with world-class orchestras is a graduate degree in classical music.

Of course, not everyone is like Brian. Many people aren't sure what they really want to do. They just know that it is not what they are doing. Time off for course-correction helps you leave behind the dull ache of doing a job that you just don't like and make room for a new passion. It creates the time and space to discover what kind of work feels right, and it can lead you in a direction you never expected.

Marco, a young lawyer, knew law wasn't his passion. After just one year, he left his high-powered law firm for a Reboot Break. His time off allowed him to explore his interest in business. Not long after the break, he founded a tech company. But his work wasn't done. Two years later he took another course-correction sabbatical. This time he followed his new dream of working in foreign policy. Today he's a policy analyst in Washington DC.

Some people try something new on their Reboot Break only to return to what they had been doing before. That doesn't mean the time was wasted. The opportunity to explore a passion can go a long way toward reducing the stress of feeling as though you've missed an opportunity or that you really should be doing something else.

Linda, a therapist, used her Reboot Break to live overseas and write, then start a small business. The business didn't succeed, but she loved trying it. Today she's returned to her work as a therapist, and in her free time she writes plays and travels.

If you are feeling as if you've handed your life over to your job, or you are resentful because you think your job is keeping you from fulfilling your dreams, a course-correction sabbatical can help you feel more satisfied or find a new direction. You might find that what you needed wasn't a career change, but the freedom to expand your life outside of work. When a passion has been ignited, sometimes the old job doesn't seem so bad, especially if it helps pay for your new hobby.

FAMILY-RELATED SABBATICAL

A family-related sabbatical may be right for you if:

- *You are finding it more and more difficult to balance your work and home life.*
- *You wish you had more time to spend with a loved one who has special needs or is ill or dying.*
- *You have family goals you aren't able to meet while working full-time.*

Nancy took a family-related sabbatical at thirty-five to have children.

My U.S. Army husband was being transferred from Washington DC to Europe, and I agreed to leave my White House national security job to accompany him. My number one goal was to start a family. Much to

our delight, we had two daughters in the next three years. I was at home
with them for their earliest years in Germany and Japan, so I had the
wonderful gift of time to bond with them.

A family-related sabbatical allows you to let go of the guilt and devote
time to the people who need you most. It may not fix all the problems, but it can give you some relief when you're feeling pulled in
too many directions. It can let you listen to your heart when it tells
you that nothing is more important than being there for the ones you
love when they truly need you. Unfortunately, our loved ones' timing
isn't always ideal. Maybe you're up for a promotion when your father
becomes ill, or your teenage daughter is failing school right after you
win the big account.

Alison took a workplace sabbatical in 1994 at age forty-eight from
her financial services firm, where she was one of the highest-ranking
officers. The primary purpose was to be more involved with her
son during the summer before he started high school. John, a high-
functioning autistic teen, was completing junior high. It had been
a tough time for him. Alison and her husband wanted to help their
son prepare to enter high school. She wanted to be with him to help
work on his coordination, self-confidence, and self-sufficiency, which
would in turn help his ability to make friends and fit in.

She took her Reboot Break as family leave under the Family and
Medical Leave Act (See Chapter 3). Her bosses were reluctant to
give her the time, but she knew they had no choice because of the
law, which was new at the time, and they ultimately agreed. Alison's
summer with her son was precious. She was with him every day, just
spending time together or doing special projects. One interesting
project they did involved sorting their closets and drawers, which
hadn't been done in years. She turned the task into a fun, joint activity
of 15–30 minutes each day to get rid of stuff as a team. She even
taught him to cook.

John blossomed into "more of a guy" as he became more coordinated
and better at sports under the tutelage of a trainer. Alison worked
with him in other ways too, such as his independence skills and how

he dressed. They took a trip to visit her dad in Nebraska, but she had John stay longer and then navigate his way home alone through two flights and a plane change. He became more self-confident and knew that he could master the change ahead of him called high school.

Returning to work, Alison felt refreshed and energized. She looks back on the Reboot Break as one of the highlights of her career and a key to a burst of energy and productivity. And, most importantly, it helped her son. Alison says, "The Reboot Break was really the right thing at the right time."

While family-related sabbaticals provide the flexibility to do what is necessary for a family member, they may also benefit the sabbatical taker. Many find the experience life changing, an impetus to reorder priorities.

After Jimmy's wife died, he and his children took a Reboot Break so they all could heal, travel, and just be together to re-establish their lives.

Sometimes people don't take their Reboot Break for family reasons, but life circumstances bring the family more into focus. Leena was on a Reboot Break when her father suffered a stroke. It was a blessing that she had the flexibility to be able to crisscross the Atlantic Ocean several times to be with him and help manage his care.

EMOTIONAL HEALING SABBATICAL

You may need an emotional healing sabbatical if:

- *You recently lost a spouse, partner, parent, child, or other loved one.*
- *You are divorced or separated from a spouse or partner.*
- *You are a survivor of an illness or situation that was traumatic or life-threatening.*
- *You recently experienced an upsetting job loss.*

Difficult emotional times are a natural part of life. Romantic relationships fall apart. People we love die. Life deals us a hand that we didn't expect, and we do our best to cope.

All the while, we're plugging away at our jobs, rushing to meetings, traveling, pushing papers. Sometimes the work is therapeutic, distracting us from our crisis. Other times we wonder how we can keep smiling at our co-workers, customers, and clients, acting as though things are okay. We need to take time off.

An emotional healing sabbatical is about nursing one's wounds and transitioning to a new "place" with lessons learned. The wounds may not be entirely gone at sabbatical's end, but time and a new understanding of life will have made them more bearable.

In her popular book—now a movie—*Eat, Pray, Love,* Elizabeth Gilbert set out to find balance in her life by taking a Reboot Break. Gilbert plumbed the depths of her soul and told the world about it. Readers are the beneficiaries of her struggles and insights, of her pain when she left her marriage and suffered through the stages of divorce. Also, she was seeking her own truth about her place in society and how she would live her life. She took refuge and sought answers in food, prayer, and love in three different countries, and eventually she found inner peace and a new understanding of herself.

In the classic book *Gift from the Sea* (1955), Anne Morrow Lindbergh's insights from her time away at the beach to seek balance are about understanding how recognizing and embracing the emotional threads of life will weave in more strength, texture, richness, and clarity. Her lessons are strikingly similar to those we have gleaned from our own Reboot Breaks and from our many interviews with both women and men.

Leena shared the story of her time on a Reboot Break. Her twenty-month sabbatical journey combined emotional healing, searching for her next job and place to live, and surprises along the way.

Leena had not planned on taking a Reboot Break, but at thirty-six, when she sold her Internet-based food delivery business in London, she realized that she needed to take time off to heal from a broken heart. So, a professional circumstance and an emotional need came together and spelled "Reboot Break." Now, she would have time to heal the wound and to figure out her next professional calling. She even called into question where she lived. Untethered from her business, she was moving into a period of being open to what could happen next, both personally and professionally.

She first returned for several months to Lebanon, where she had grown up. She had been away for fourteen years, except for short visits, and longed for the beautiful Lebanese mountains and exciting Beirut. Leena wanted to catch up with the family and friends she missed so much. She hadn't realized how low she had sunk emotionally and was thankful for the time away from daily routine and work pressures to heal. It helped so much to be back in the nurturing bosom of family and friends. She read self-help books, practiced yoga, and worked on moving past that "dark place." She began to feel more hopeful about the future.

Leena traveled to Madrid to stay with friends. There, she took a painting and drawing class, which she had always wanted to do. She worked on improving her Spanish, too, which enabled her to start meeting new people and building new relationships. The more time she spent in Madrid, the more she began to see that this would be a good place for her to live. An interesting work idea came along, and she began to make concrete plans to move to Madrid.

With this newfound direction and plan, Leena returned to London to sell her apartment and gather her things for the move. As luck or kismet would have it, she met someone while back in London. His name was José. She found herself facing the kind of situation that happens to many a sabbatical taker. Because she had opened herself up to life in a new way, she now was presented with a new opportunity—and the challenge of thinking deeply about what was truly important to her. She felt torn and had to decide what she was going to do: continue in an orderly fashion with her plan to move to Madrid, or explore her relationship with José.

Leena, the former "strictly business" businesswoman, followed her heart. It helped that she was still on her Reboot Break. She had the flexibility to shelve the Madrid plan and extend her time away from work. The relationship blossomed and, after a time, she and José married and now live in the Washington DC area.

Leena's experience demonstrates that taking the time to reflect and allow for new thoughts, ideas, and experiences can enrich life with new possibilities. In more dramatic terms, one could say that taking time off can nudge the unfolding of one's destiny, one's future. Leena is certain that without her Reboot Break, she would not have been open to building a relationship with José. First, her heart may not have healed. Second, she would have been tied to a job that would not have afforded her the time to explore and pursue the relationship and discover what she really wanted and needed.

Leena also transformed her view of work and changed her career direction. She now works at a non-profit organization, and her life's work—her found passion—is promoting better understanding between Muslims and non-Muslims and being involved in peace projects in the Middle East.

VOLUNTEERING SABBATICAL

A volunteering sabbatical may be right for you if:

- *You long to make a difference in the lives of others.*
- *You have a particular skill you'd like to use to make the world a better place.*
- *You want to travel to distant lands, but traveling as a "tourist" doesn't appeal to you.*

Rita says that volunteer work has always been one of her passions. It took a Reboot Break to satisfy her desire to become more deeply involved.

In the past several years when I was working eighteen-hour days and traveling constantly, something had to give, and it was my ability to commit time to volunteering. Though I contributed financially to several non-profit organizations and was on the board of one, I started to crave spending more time on work that seemed so important to me. I was quickly coming to the conclusion that I needed to make volunteering my work, rather than having it be the thing I did on top of a full day. When my company announced that it was moving its headquarters to another part of the country, it was the perfect time to take a Reboot Break.

I used the time to immerse myself in microfinance, a field where the results are immediate, tangible, and scalable. I was soon asked to become chair of Pro Mujer, a non-profit organization that gives $170 loans to women in Latin America whose families earn under $2 a day. Pro Mujer also provides business and self-esteem training and health services for the whole family. The 99.9 percent repayment rate shows that there is a real need.

I felt good about my efforts and contributions. I was able to bring my business knowledge and experience to bear on several strategic areas for the organization. But I felt even better when I traveled to our banks. Before doing so, I enrolled in Spanish classes so that I could converse with our clients. I complemented the classes at home with Spanish immersion weeks in Antigua, Guatemala, and Oaxaca, Mexico. I traveled to our existing programs in Bolivia, Nicaragua, Peru, and Mexico and went with the founders to Argentina to set up a new program.

My life is so much more enriched by all the women I have had a chance to meet. I cried when hearing their stories, with tears for the hardship of their lives and tears of happiness for their successes.

Many people long to spend time volunteering. They want to contribute in some personal way to making the world a better place, to making a difference in the face of relentless problems. Many of us take a weekday night or Saturday afternoon to mentor a child or clean litter from a highway or debris from a rundown part of town. But some of us want to spend more time and have a stronger engagement. A volunteering sabbatical can be the answer.

For us and many of our interviewees, the break was a time to give back, in small ways and large. Some of us served on non-profit boards, while others wanted the more hands-on experience of feeding the homeless in their own communities, providing medical care in Africa, or establishing schools at home or abroad.

Volunteering sabbaticals can change people in profound ways. Sometimes the transition back to your old life can be jarring. When

Nigel returned to his law firm in the UK after volunteering with his wife in Trinidad and Tobago and Ecuador, he deeply questioned his priorities and those of his colleagues. Sitting at his desk, he couldn't help but think, is all this really that important? Others were so changed by their volunteer experiences that they quit the corporate world altogether for a life of non-profit work and volunteering.

A number of corporations encourage their employees to take volunteering sabbaticals, which gives the employees rewarding experiences and the company a way to contribute to social responsibility.

The "new volunteerism" is a rapidly growing industry of customized travel programs and accommodations in places around the world where you pay to volunteer. It combines cultural and learning experiences with making a positive impact. Many websites offer listings of meaningful volunteer opportunities for people who want to give back during their Reboot Break. (See Resources in the Appendix and further discussion of volunteering in Chapters 3 and 6.)

LIFE-ENHANCEMENT SABBATICAL

You may be ready for a life-enhancement sabbatical if you:

- *Feel uninspired by your work or your life.*
- *Feel out of touch with your dreams and interests.*
- *Feel the need to connect to life's deeper meeting through spiritual exploration.*
- *Just crave meaningful time for yourself.*

Although Jaye's Reboot Break captures elements of several sabbatical types, life-enhancement was her primary objective.

I had started and built a company with three partners. Four years later, one of them retired, which caused me to take on roles and responsibilities that I didn't enjoy. And I enjoyed doing it twelve hours a day even less! After six years of forcing myself, I finally raised my hand to make a major change. Not only was I unhappy with what I was doing, I had lost touch with those I cared most about, and especially myself. I needed a break. On sabbatical, I was able to have enriching experiences that were otherwise elusive: see long-lost friends, spend quality time with family, and travel a lot to reconnect and to rediscover myself.

Reboot Breaks don't have to be motivated by a deep need or noble purpose. There may be no trauma to recover from or ambition to follow. Sometimes a Reboot Break happens just because you want to take some time for yourself and see what it feels like to stop working for a while.

Geoff told us about his experience.

My Reboot Break was a journey within myself. I had taken time off of work in my thirties to search for a better work/life balance. I started to think about how I wanted to structure my life in the future. In my travels, I met up with an old friend who had moved to Australia. I proudly told this self-made man who had retired at thirty-five that I had just been made a vice president. He responded, "That's great. So tell me, are you happy?" I spent the rest of my break working on how I could be certain to answer that question "Yes." I don't have all the answers, but I'm closer. I learned that you don't need to come out of a Reboot Break with all the perfect answers. It's okay to just recharge your batteries.

Life-enhancement sabbaticals often have an important dose of spiritual enlightenment as people seek ways to nourish their souls and get to know themselves better. It can be in small doses or as a major focus. On Marco's two course-correction sabbaticals, he felt that introspection was the most important activity. "Without logging a lot of time with myself on sabbatical, I never would have been able to figure out the career that will sustain me through my life. I learned about how I want to live my life and conduct my relationships by undertaking a search for my own spirituality. That was important and satisfying."

Many sabbatical takers find their path to self-discovery through yoga, meditation, and participating in weekend or longer programs that guide them through a process of self-reflection and spiritual exploration. **Many people are hungry for a connection to a part of themselves that is untapped and under-celebrated.** Some also want to feel connected to a larger spiritual community of like-minded people to help support them.

PRE-RETIREMENT SABBATICAL

A pre-retirement sabbatical may be right for you if:

- *You want to "test the waters" of retired life.*
- *You know you'll need to work during retirement and want to figure out what kind of work you'd like to do.*
- *You know what you want to do during your retirement—you're going to start a business or build a house or become a yoga instructor—and you want to get a head start on your plans.*

Cathy's sabbatical in 2007 was a pre-retirement sabbatical.

I, like many Baby Boomers, was not ready to retire. Rather, I see myself working well into my seventies, but with more time for other things. I wanted more control over my work life and to follow some of the passions and dreams I had left behind in my last career phase.

I used the eight months off to get more involved with philanthropy and work behind the scenes on fundraising and policy development for a presidential campaign. I continued to give presentations in the financial services and technology fields so that I kept up connections and continued to learn.

The most exciting parts of the time off were closer to my passions of travel and design. I was building a new guest house on my property in Santa Fe and loved every minute of the planning. I also traded houses with an acquaintance and spent a month in France with friends, some from my business connections. What gelled from those two experiences was how to use my guesthouse and house in Santa Fe as places for talented and engaged people to meet and work on some of the problems facing the United States in its need to be globally competitive. I'm back at the Santa Fe Group now, working on how to turn that thought into a business opportunity.

As people approach retirement age, they often begin to think about what they will do in retirement and want to position themselves for it. A pre-retirement sabbatical in your fifties or sixties can help you explore what to do later. You may look forward to the extra time and freedom of retirement and want a taste of it in advance. Or you may contemplate retirement with some trepidation and want to lay some groundwork for it. A pre-retirement sabbatical can be used to try volunteering, take a class or an extended trip, start a hobby, or anything else that offers a taste of what may be in store after leaving a full-time career. A pre-retirement sabbatical can be taken either from the workplace or between gigs.

PHASED RETIREMENT: THE NEW WAY

Baby Boomers and others are foregoing old-fashioned retirement. Instead of ending their careers only to spend their time in leisure, they are increasingly spending their post-retirement years working part-time or volunteering. There are seventy-eight million Baby Boomers in their sixties now, at or near traditional retirement age, but polls indicate that only about thirty percent actually plan to quit work. And the number of those who plan to keep working at least part-time is growing, according to a 2008 Gallup poll. Some of this is financial necessity, but some of it is simply not wanting to retire.

We call this new lifestyle that pairs traditional retirement's relaxation and discovery with rewarding work "phased retirement." It's a term we have borrowed from law firms, which have a long and enlightened tradition of allowing their older associates and partners, like Sam, to cut back their work without leaving the firm. An attorney in his sixties, Sam is still a partner but he spends most of his time working on pro bono cases and mentoring the firm's younger employees.

For some, phased retirement means leaving an old job behind for new, more interesting work. Dick "retired" from an active legal career at sixty-five. After some time off, he became a volunteer with the Baltimore Symphony Orchestra. Today he heads the orchestra's youth outreach program.

The new gig may be the realization of an old dream (even a reinvention), or a different incarnation of the previous career. Often, it fulfills a desire to use one's lifetime of personal and work skills in volunteering. Roberta, a retired banker, volunteers her financial skills, helping young entrepreneurs prepare their taxes. Frank, a retired government worker, donates his legal expertise at a nearby homeless shelter.

Many people don't realize they want a phased retirement until after they retire. They have the idea that being on vacation—for the rest of their life!—will be nothing but bliss. And for some it is.

But after six months, a year, or maybe two, many think to themselves, *Is this all there is?*

Kevin, an Idaho entrepreneur and professor, knew he wasn't ready for traditional retirement. But he was ready to find a better balance between his work and personal life. At sixty, he resigned from his last full-time job and took time off to figure out the right balance of work and personal time, as well as the kind of work he could do that would be satisfying. Today Kevin spends three days a week counseling small business entrepreneurs and teaches one college-level business course. He also manages an "angel fund" that he created to help entrepreneurs who want to start new companies and serves as a governor of the Rotary Club.

"I'm doing these things because I have the time now," Kevin said. "The angel fund keeps me connected to that community. Being the Rotary Club governor is a labor of love, and I have talent to bring to it. It's a gift that I have time to do all of this."

Phased retirement can take many different forms. And it is truly changing the way people live their lives in their older years. Marc Freedman, in his book *Encore: Finding Work That Matters in the Second Half of Life*, talks about what we all have to gain from people who seek active and purposeful lives long after our parents stepped off life's stage.

▶ EXERCISES

Exercise 2-1: Your Motivations

- Which type of sabbatical(s) do you identify with most?
- Write down the issue or motivation driving you toward one or more of the types of sabbaticals.
- Think about the direct impact a Reboot Break break could have, and make lists of the pros and cons.

CHAPTER 3

It's All in the Planning

"A goal without a plan is just a wish."

—*Antoine de Saint-Exupéry*

Congratulations! Now that you've decided to take a Reboot Break, it's time to put together a plan to help you to make the most of it. Whether you are a non-planner, a great planner, or an over-planner, this chapter will provide you with helpful insights on:

- The crucial role that planning plays.
- How to pre-empt potential emotional hurdles about planning.
- How to prepare for conversations with bosses, spouses, and children.
- The tactical steps you will need to consider in advance for a successful break.
- How planning can also enable entrepreneurs, sole practitioners, and small business owners to take time off.
- Resources that will help in planning and giving you the "gift of time." (Understanding the ways in which you can fund your time off is so important that we have dedicated a full chapter—Chapter

4—to the multitude of options and resources available to anyone considering taking time off.)

No sabbatical dreams come true by happenstance. Each dream is unique and needs first to be imagined, then planned and implemented by the one person who can do it . . . you!

WHY PLANNING IS IMPORTANT AND WHY IT'S SOMETIMES HARD

Planning is the key for everyone taking a Reboot Break. It enables you to fulfill your goals, expectations, and needs for this time-off period. It lays the groundwork, ensuring that you will get the most from the sabbatical experience. It helps determine the resources needed, the things that need to be put in place, and at what stage. It leads one to think about contingencies and to be better prepared.

We recommend starting six months to a year ahead of your Reboot Break, but many people plan successfully on shorter notice. Others choose to plan several years ahead. Every situation is unique. The trick is to leave enough flexibility to be spontaneous and open to learning lessons along the way, but at the same time to think through enough details in advance to make sure opportunities are not lost.

Eileen planned a year in advance of taking a twelve-month Reboot Break, starting with a list of her goals, which included travel and reconnecting with friends. Although she had a terrific time and enjoyed her trip to France and Switzerland, she later regretted that she hadn't planned more of the specifics. She had wanted to take cooking classes in France, for example, but missed the opportunity because it needed to be researched and reserved in advance.

There is creative tension between planning and not planning, being over-programmed and not being programmed enough. The objective is to have structure to achieve your goals but also leave lots of downtime and room for flexibility and opportunity. Planning also does not come easily to everyone. What keeps us from planning?

- Many of us are procrastinators.
- We have lingering emotions of fear or guilt about taking time off.
- It feels easier to us to just let things happen.
- We just don't know how to plan.

All of these circumstances are normal, but they must be overcome. Push past these inhibitors and get started.

PLANNING BASICS

Here are some basics for anyone starting to plan for a time away:

- Identify your major goals.
- Decide how much time to take. If it is an unexpected sabbatical, figure out how flexible you can be with time off.
- Figure out what financial and other resources you will need.
- Decide what you will need to do ahead of time to be able to take time off.
- Determine whom to tell, who will be impacted, and how you will deal with that.
- If you are an entrepreneur or sole practitioner, decide what planning is needed well in advance.
- Decide whether travel is included, and if so, what advance planning is needed.
- Do a plan outline and timelines for the Reboot Break period.
- Identify fears that might get in the way and how to address them.
- Schedule down time for yourself. If your goal is to get off the racetrack and smell the roses, then carving out time for yourself to think, reflect, and feel can be enough of a plan, at least for the beginning of a Reboot Break.

* * *

GETTING STARTED: IDENTIFYING GOALS

Here are some preliminary steps you might take in identifying your major goals and outcomes:

1. Think and daydream about your time off.
2. Write about it, which makes it more real.
3. Talk about it to others to get reinforcement.
4. Write down steps to take toward those dreams.

You know yourself. Think carefully about what you need to do to feel afterward that you made the best use of your break and special time off. What are the categories of things you would like to do? Do you have a major, overarching goal, like getting an MBA, traveling to Asia, or running a marathon? If so, what do you need to do to accomplish that? What are some of your other goals, large and small, and how might you reach them?

Laura needed a break from her high-stress job. She and her husband had dreamed about traveling internationally during the ten years of their marriage. He had found a summer project assignment in Australia, and now here was their chance to realize those dreams. She jumped at the opportunity to take a leave of absence and join him. Together they planned what they would do and how they would do it. That was half the fun. They got their kids involved and planned places they wanted to see, activities they wanted to do, and what their budget might be. The kids each had research assignments around those activities and places, and Laura and her husband used the time to broaden their kids' knowledge as well as their own.

We suggest several techniques for helping the creative process:

Visualize—Movement assists in thinking more creatively and boldly because it allows the mind to shift from the left side of the brain to the right side, which enables you to be open to new possibilities. We recommend taking a walk in a calm and peaceful place, such as a park or by the water—somewhere where you won't be distracted—to contemplate your time off. Spend at least thirty minutes permitting your mind to go to a place that allows it to stretch and imagine the ideal. Assume there are no barriers. Let yourself imagine what your ideal break would look and feel like. Make a point of not talking to anyone while on this walking/visualization exercise. Later, when you return to a place where you can write, get those ideas down in a journal uncensored.

Jaye used the visualization technique to plan her Reboot Break. It included how she would tell her partner she was leaving the business, what she would say to clients, and, more importantly, what she wanted to do when she had the time off. This included everything from addressing health issues to exploring a new career path. It worked for her.

On the other hand, Ned didn't take the time to visualize before he began his six-month sabbatical. All he knew was that he was tired and overwhelmed and needed an emotional break. He began to realize when his time off was coming to an end that he never did the things he would have liked to do. He hadn't planned for them. He is now a strong advocate for planning and is, in fact, planning his next sabbatical.

Think Boldly—Zoe at age twenty-five left her job at an environmental organization after months of dreaming of doing the St. James pilgrimage in Spain. After discussion with colleagues, plus a lot of planning, she embarked on a complex ten-month travel sabbatical. Her planning included where she wanted to go, what it took to do the pilgrimage, whether her friends would be available to visit, what experiences she wanted to have, and a budget. She did the pilgrimage in Spain, hiking the Pyrenees Mountains along the famed 480-mile Camino del Compostela, also called the Way of St. James. Then she stayed on in Spain for a few months, taking Spanish classes. Next she traveled to Germany, living with friends for two months. Then she was off to northern Thailand before trekking in Nepal. She finished her travel living on a French farm for the last three months. The experience led her to the field of conflict resolution, a master's degree, and a new career.

Without a bold step in life, some things would never be. Surround yourself with pictures, articles, books, and inspiring quotes. Make a collage with images of all the places you want to go and things you want to do, and hang it by your desk or bed to remind you of your dreams.

Talk to Others—If you don't have a clear idea of your life goals or Reboot Break goals, you can talk to others. By verbalizing your thoughts and ideas, especially with someone who will give you encouragement, you make them more real and achievable. Beyond family and friends, blogs are one way to do this. Please join us at our blog on *www.reboot yourlifebook.com*. Another way is creating or joining a community, such as our Reboot Your Life groups on Facebook and LinkedIn. Another example is the community we have created through the retreats we hold, with the attendees staying in touch afterward.

Write It Down—Putting pen to paper is another way to start to turn dreams into reality. Journaling about your thoughts right from the start is an excellent way to capture ideas, fears, and wishes—all a significant part of the planning process. Maybe you already write in a journal daily, or maybe you never have. Grab your journal or a handy notebook or go out and buy a blank book for writing, and then sit in a quiet place to think and write. Research has shown that there's a greater connection between the paper and the mind when writing by hand as opposed to using a computer.

DECIDING HOW LONG TO TAKE OFF

If you are taking a between-gigs sabbatical or are out of work on an unexpected sabbatical, you still need to plan a timeframe for your sabbatical and for returning to work. The length of time you stay on your Reboot Break most likely will relate to your financial resources. We advise making a conscious decision to plan a Reboot Break after losing a job and not to seek a new job right away. We recommend planning at least a three-month break, if possible, plus having an additional three months in financial reserves in case the job search takes longer than anticipated once you begin it. If you can take a longer break, such as six months to a year, go for it.

If you are working, your company's policies will influence how long you can take off. Does the company have a sabbatical or leave-of-absence policy, and would it work for you? How long does it allow? Is it paid or unpaid? If there is no policy, has anyone else ever asked to take a sabbatical? Has anyone taken time off without pay and been able to return to the company and his or her same job? These are questions your human resources department can help you to answer. You might also speak to longtime employees who may have taken advantage of some of these benefits.

Other factors in deciding how long a Reboot Break to take may include:

- How long you think it will take to achieve all you dream about doing.
- How much time you need to accomplish a specific goal, such as an academic program.
- How much time your company provides.
- How much time you can afford to take off financially.
- A season or specific period of time, such as summer when the kids are out of school.
- Requirements of a specific program, such as the Family and Medical Leave Act, or any other program in which you might be participating.

The Family and Medical Leave Act (FMLA) is designed to assist people needing time to tend to medical issues for a family member. Should your Reboot Break be focused on caring for an ill family member, you can take up to three months off, intermittently or all at once. You must have proof of the illness and the relationship to get approval.

Dorothy's daughter, Shanna, gave birth to her first child. All had gone well but the baby was born prematurely. Shanna was living at home at the time, with Dorothy and her husband. While Dorothy was thrilled to have her first grandchild come into the world, she knew that her daughter was not prepared to care for her new baby alone. With Dorothy's very demanding job running a child welfare agency, there was little time for her own family and to support her daughter. Dorothy researched and discovered that she could take advantage of the FMLA to assist her daughter and new grandchild.

Dorothy was able to take two weeks at first and then three weeks intermittently over the next two months to spend time with her new grandchild. She was thrilled to have this special time with him, to support her daughter, and to get away from the distractions of her busy job.

Ben's mother was diagnosed with Alzheimer's. He wanted to help her to get her life in order and get her settled somewhere where she would feel well taken care of and comfortable. He asked for, and received, a three-month FMLA leave. He used the break to spend quality time with his mother but also to clean out her house, sell it, and get her settled somewhere safe. He loved being with her and was able to take care of her proactively while also giving himself the "gift of time" with her. It gave him a sense of relief and peace to know that she was where she needed to be.

Sometimes people end up extending their Reboot Break if they can, either because they aren't ready to return to a more structured routine, or because they feel they just haven't yet accomplished what they set out to do. For those with the flexibility, extending the time away is a great option.

Mary Pat had originally planned to take eight months off when she resigned from her senior-level marketing position. She planned a number of things to do during this time of healing and exploration. As she approached the eight-month mark, she realized that she had much more to do and that the doors had just started opening up for her. Going back to a full-time work routine felt counterproductive and premature; she had already invested considerable time to get where she was. While on her Reboot Break, Mary Pat was approached by a number of recruiters. Since she still wasn't ready to return to full-time work, she turned the opportunities into some consulting assignments to rebuild her financial resources. Then she joyfully continued her break. Today, Mary Pat is consulting and still leaving more time for herself. She integrated what she learned from her time off to move into a career that gave her more control over where she lived, what she did, and how much time she worked.

What If You Were Taking a Year Off?

Susan started charting her course in her late twenties, twelve months ahead of the year-long sabbatical she planned to take from her job in banking. Susan knew that she was planning for the next stage of her life and wanted to be thoughtful about what she was doing. She applied to a six-month academic program in England, then requested and received permission from her employer to attend and extend the time off to a year. "I knew that I needed a full year," she said, "and I know that when I have things planned, I am more productive and get more out of my time away. If you don't plan, time escapes you and the things you had dreamed of fade away."

More and more people are taking a full year off in order to achieve a longer-term life shift. Many people travel for a year and leave their creature comforts behind. Some volunteer during their time away. Studying often requires a commitment of at least a year for career enhancement or to acquire enough knowledge for a career shift and to be more credible.

We recommend a year or more break to truly get the impact and lasting benefits of being away, but any amount of time away is nourishing and recharging. For those of you still uncertain about taking a longer break, mini-sabbaticals are a good way to test the waters.

Starting Out Small: Testing the Waters

Starting with a long Reboot Break can be daunting, in terms of planning, financing, or facing fears. In a down economy, small steps may seem more palatable. Although we recommend that Reboot Breaks ideally last several months to a year, one suggestion is trying a shorter "mini-sabbatical," to pave the way. You can try taking a break for a few days to a month. Structured the right way, a weekend, a week, or a month can give you a glimpse of what a real stretch of time can do.

Some people try something or someplace new for a short time and then decide whether they want to pursue the activity on a more sustained basis or go back to the place for longer.

For some people, taking a long weekend to unplug from the Black-Berry and computer and be alone with no schedule offers a small test of what it would be like to take a Reboot Break. A mini-sabbatical can also test the logistical and emotional planning required with one's family or significant other, the financial resources needed, how the office will get along without you, whether you can handle simply being alone for a period of time, and ways of overcoming feelings of guilt.

Will left his work as a photographer in New York City for the month of March to refresh his soul, mind, and spirit. "It was an imperative for me. I had to do it. You have to do this kind of thing for yourself. You have to work it out financially and figure out how long you can take. I scheduled my photography jobs so I could be gone, and I went to Texas with my camera in hand just for pleasure. I drove for one month all over the state, loving not working, listening to music, taking pictures."

When Cathy traded houses to spend a month in Italy in 2006, it went so smoothly with her staff in her absence that she realized her real sabbatical could be much longer than the three months she had planned.

Cathy and others offer some good advice about planning mini-sabbaticals:

- **Unplugging can be the hardest part.** Tell your office and others ahead of time that you are not going to be available electronically. Then try to stick to that plan to get the most out of your time off.
- **You can do a lot in a month.** It's twice the time of a two-week vacation and twice the opportunity to get away from it all and relax or try something new. Planning helps you make the most of it.

- **Involve your family in the planning and—if it fits the plan—in the mini-sabbatical itself.** It should be a time to get away from normal chores and routines.
- **You can be creative without spending huge amounts of money.** For example, some people trade houses or even house-sit for a short period of time. That gets them away from their routine and into position to explore new places. The web can be helpful in identifying opportunities.
- **Plan ahead, starting with making a list of things you have been wanting to do.** Figure out how to make it happen.

In Chapter 10, Living the Lifelong Sabbatical, we talk more about ideas and tips for mini-sabbaticals and how they can be a lifelong practice.

WHOM TO TELL AND HOW: PLANNING CONVERSATIONS

Make a list of all the people who will be impacted by your taking time off. Start with your family members, friends, and others who count on you. Then list employers, colleagues, clients, and customers. Include any corporate or not-for-profit boards you may be on or community projects in which you are engaged. Plan what to tell them, and when.

TALKING TO YOUR SPOUSE/PARTNER, CHILDREN, AND FRIENDS

Your transition will be smoother if you include, early in the planning process, the people who will be affected by your taking a Reboot Break. They can be sounding boards and challenge you to think more—or less—broadly. Fearing the reactions of others and thus avoiding those potentially difficult conversations will cause more problems than dealing with them up front in a calm and confident way. If you are convinced of your decision, others will get on board more quickly, especially if you ask for their help, support, and ideas. If you receive some pushback from naysayers, don't let them rain on your parade. (We talk more about reactions of loved ones in Chapter 9.)

When a spouse or partner is a co-sabbatical taker, it is even more important to share each other's goals and expectations and to find alignment and build a plan that suits both of you.

Barry wanted to take three months off from his position as leader of a synagogue. He felt it was important to take time to reflect and learn something new to bring back to his congregation. He started planning for the time off with the help and involvement of his wife, Sarah. She worked as a teacher and needed to plan long in advance if she was to participate in any way. Together they made a list of what they each wanted to accomplish during this time away. It was important for both of them to come back refreshed and armed with a fresh outlook and new perspectives. They each took courses that had been on their list and took three two-week vacations away together. Their unexpected gift from this time together was that it reinforced their own relationship and strengthened it.

Children, too, need to be a part of the conversation, once you are clear and have a plan. They will want to know what to expect and how it will affect them. At the same time, you can leave room for their additions and suggestions. From the mouths of children can come creative, unfettered thoughts, ideas, and possibilities.

Talk to your friends. They may provide just the encouragement, support, and ideas you need.

Getting Your Employer on Board

Now that you have decided to take a Reboot Break, you need to get your employer on board. Employers want to have energized and productive staff members, so there is something in this for your boss as well as for you. You might approach it that way in your discussions.

"Are you crazy?" you ask. "You don't know my boss. This would be impossible at my company." Well, you may just be surprised, and you'll never know if you don't ask. If you are working for a small company or a start-up and you and your colleagues are in the throes of launching the company, new products, or a new line of business, then the timing may not be right for you. It's up to you to pick the right time, communicate it, and plan well in advance for it.

Bill was the VP of a major business line at a top computer company, and he was planning to start a two-month sabbatical within days of the most important product launch in the company's history. As the head of this major business, the lifeline of the company, how could he disconnect completely for two months when the product had to be flawless and there were major customers and analyst meetings to be had? Besides that, the company had no sabbatical program and no one had ever taken a sabbatical.

Bill explained to those who wondered how he could do it that he had made a personal resolution to take two months off to be with his family every three years in the summertime. He started communicating his resolve three years ahead of time, telling his boss, the CEO, and co-workers that "in three years time I will be taking two months off." Of course, no one paid any attention to him for something that was so far off. Every six months he reminded everyone of his plans. As the time got closer, he reminded people every month and created a plan so that his employees were empowered and prepared to run the business. The launch went off flawlessly and catapulted the company. He had a wonderful time refreshing himself and reconnecting with his wife and his teenage children as they traveled and explored Europe.

Maybe you work for a very small company and you and your co-workers are each doing the work of three people. Again, timing is everything. This may simply not be the time to ask, but that doesn't mean that you give up your dream. The people who get the most out of a Reboot Break dream about it and plan for it a year or more ahead of time. If you were suddenly taken ill or if you are a woman and became pregnant, even small companies would give you time off—six weeks in the case of a maternity break—and they survive. You may want to start with a mini break of two or three weeks, but share with your boss your desire and your resolve to be able to take a longer Reboot Break someday.

We've spoken to many lawyers who have said there is no way a lawyer can take a sabbatical or Reboot Break. They claim that their clients depend on the individual client-attorney relationship and would never accept a replacement. Others point to the partner revenue sharing as an obstacle, feeling that it wouldn't be fair to take off two or three months. But many well recognized and well run law firms successfully offer sabbatical programs. They have found a way to handle these objections and claim that their programs work well for lawyers and for the clients. For a list of some law firms and other entities offering programs, see the Appendix "Organizations That Get It."

Be sure to prepare for your conversation with your boss. It is important to be clear that this is something you want and need to do, that you have thought through how your work can be managed during your absence, and that you have a reentry plan that will enable you to transition back with little or no interruption in the business. Thus, the benefits will clearly outweigh any negative concerns.

Making the Business Case

We suggest scripting the conversation so that you don't miss valuable points in presenting the business case, not just your case. As you approach your conversation, it might be helpful for you and your boss to know that many successful companies and organizations are offering sabbaticals. We have researched or talked to 150 corporations, law firms, non-profits, trade associations, government agencies, and small enterprises that offer sabbaticals or otherwise support employees who want to take time off. Some of these organizations have formal sabbatical programs with paid leave, and some just allow people to have a job waiting when they return. Some organizations cover their employees' healthcare benefits while they're not working or offer the insurance at the company rate.

Employers are more willing to help those desiring a Reboot Break because they see the value to the organization's culture, recruitment, retention, and capacity to innovate. Sabbaticals are also fundamental to building the breadth and depth of employees within the organization, both those who take them and those who fill in. The latter become more experienced and flexible by standing in for the absent colleague, and the organization builds resilience.

In 2009 there were nineteen companies on Fortune's "100 Best Companies to Work For" that sponsored sabbatical programs, a 36 percent increase on 2008. Our research suggests that the trend is in fact on the rise. Some companies—such as AARP, American Express, Charles Schwab, Deloitte, eBay, Intel, McDonalds, Newsweek, Random House, Inc., Scholastic, and Text 100—have offered one- to three-month paid sabbaticals. Others, like the consulting firm Accenture, help employees set aside part of their paychecks to finance a three-month leave, with a continuation of benefits.

The trend toward sabbaticals has remained true even during the economic downturn, with the added innovation of furloughing to keep employees but cut costs. Furloughing is somewhat common, with employees being asked to take a month or even a year off with reduced pay or even no pay. They get to refresh and come back reinvigorated and rededicated as even stronger employees. Some law firms are encouraging first-year associates to delay coming to the firm and instead do volunteer work for three to six months, and most firms are paying them partial salaries to do so.

Given the business advantages of granting sabbaticals to employees, you can make a strong business case to your employer. Here are some points you might want to make:

- **Sabbaticals and taking time off are the state-of-the-art way to energize talent and build leadership skills.** Leaders and managers need to take a step back and away to refuel themselves to bring that renewed energy back to the organization.
- **Sabbaticals enhance staff capabilities and succession planning for those who remain behind.** These employees get the opportunity to step up and stretch their capabilities. They can have more visibility and lay the groundwork for their own future advancement in the organization.

- **Sabbaticals induce loyalty.** Employees who are allowed time off for rebooting are more likely to stay in the organization longer, lowering turnover and recruitment costs.
- **Returning employees are usually healthier and happier**, improving company morale and lowering healthcare costs.

When asking for the time off, be prepared to talk about why it is important for you to take the time off, what you plan to do, and then— more importantly for your employer—the benefits to them. When going in to negotiate your time off, be prepared to discuss what your ideal break would include. Can you get salary continuation? How will health benefits be covered? If they are not paid for by your company, make sure that you personally contribute so that your health insurance is not interrupted. Check that this Reboot Break is treated as a leave of absence and does not create an interruption in years of service for things like future vacation accrual, pensions, 401(k), etc.

Having a conversation with employers and managers doesn't have to be difficult. Mary, who you may recall from Chapter 1 was desperate to take a break, approached the human resources department at her commodity-trading company first to test the waters. There was no sabbatical leave policy, and no one would dream that a trader would ask for time off. But, they were supportive and gave her some valuable advice about how to approach her manager. Following their suggestions, she offered to help train someone to step temporarily into her shoes, thereby increasing that employee's abilities. She explained why she needed a sabbatical and the benefits she hoped to gain from it. The manager wasn't thrilled, but considering the costs of finding someone of Mary's caliber to replace her, the manager decided she was worth waiting for and gave her the go-ahead. (Chapter 1 has other relevant examples and information on workplace sabbaticals.)

You can prepare your employer by making a strong argument for yourself and for the business case. The more in tune you are to what is in it for them to agree to your taking this time away, the more likely they are to agree. At the same time, once employers or business partners see your commitment, it is harder for them to turn down the idea. Think about whether you want to return to the same job in the organization or have flexibility to move to something new, and be prepared to discuss that.

Go into the meeting with a well thought-out plan about the delegation of your work load, the timeframe, the benefits to you, and the potential benefits to the company. Including other managers in your decision and in the design of how to handle things during your sabbatical will help smooth the transition. Acknowledge their advice and make sure they feel heard, but never let them derail the plan. Reinforce the benefits to them, the employees, and clients.

If the business case doesn't work, there is always the business proposition approach. Dale says she got time off from her job in New Zealand for her sabbatical by "striking a deal" with her boss on how the work would get done:

"I had to produce two major reports before leaving (a huge task) and one when I got back. I basically worked a few seventy-hour weeks before going and on my return. I also arranged for a friend of mine to work part-time to cover me while I was away. But it was worth it in the end. The time off really energized me."

Announcement

Make your boss's life easier. Here is a sample email announcement to your organization regarding your planned time off. You can decide with your boss if the letter comes from you or from your boss. There are a number of ways to approach this; this is one option:

Dear colleagues and staff,

Many of you are aware that I will be taking advantage of the company's sabbatical program this summer. I will be away from xxxx to xxxx. While I am away you will be able to speak to xxxx, who has been fully brought up to speed on all the projects in which I am involved and can answer any of your questions to help move things forward in my absence. You will find him/her insightful and well prepared. I appreciate your support of our mutual projects during my absence and look forward to returning in xxx, energized and ready to jump back in to carry on our work together. I am available for questions or concerns up until my leave begins on xxx.

Thank you.

Talking to Co-Workers, Peers, Board Members

This needs to be handled with care. Some co-workers may be resentful or jealous and might in some way try to undermine your plan. Being sensitive to their feelings is critical for the success of the plan. They will want to feel included and considered, and they will want to know what part they will play in your absence.

Reactions vary. Many people reported that although their co-workers were a little jealous, they also cheered them on and felt encouraged that they too could take time off later.

Make a personal call to all of the critical people in groups with which you interact regularly to share the plan for your time off and to answer any questions they might have. You don't want to surprise anyone. A clear memo to everyone a week or two before your departure, outlining who will be handling what, how to reach key people, and reassuring them that the business will be well handled during this time, is very important for maintaining your reputation and keeping the organization and your responsibilities moving forward.

Talking to Clients and Customers

Planning ahead is critical in making a smooth transition both out of your role and then later back into it, whether you are working in a corporation or have your own business. Your clients and customers need to know with confidence that their needs will be met, so providing them with information in advance will ease their minds and help insure that they will be there when you return.

Most people have had very positive reactions from clients and customers. Many have built even better relationships as a result because of how the sabbatical period was communicated, planned, and handled throughout the process. Unknowns breed fear and concern, so communicate in advance and make it clear when you will return and reenter their lives and businesses.

PLANNING FOR ENTREPRENEURS AND SOLE PRACTITIONERS

Doctors, accountants, and other professional specialists face their own unique set of issues. Many we interviewed were daunted at first at even considering a sabbatical. "How will customers, patients, and clients feel if I am not available?" "Will I lose my business if I am not there to captain the ship?" "No one will do it the way I would do it."

A striking number of people we interviewed fit into this category of having no obvious replacement during a time of leave. They all overcame their fears, took successful Reboot Breaks, and were able to return to their business or practice.

The good and bad news is that someone *can* do what you do, maybe even as well. Think of colleagues who could take your patients or customers temporarily in your full role or perhaps a reduced role. Consider hiring someone to do it as a freelance employee, asking people you trust for recommendations.

Two friends who each ran very small businesses made a deal with one another. They didn't know each other's business, but they were both successful entrepreneurs and knew how to service customers, listen, solve problems, and keep employee morale high. The two agreed to take a Reboot Break a year apart. Each would be the guardian/mentor to the person or team left in charge while the boss was away. They did so by occasionally attending meetings, as a board member might, and then during their friend's break they talked to the manager in charge at least once a week. Good leaders know how to ask good questions regardless of industry and business. They made sure they each had a good number two who could step up to run the day-to-day part of the business.

As you consider who will carry out or support your functions while you are away, plan how to train and empower them as necessary. It will be a test of your succession planning—and ability to take future Reboot Breaks—if you can work this out.

If you cannot figure out someone to take over while you are away, think about whether your customers, clients, or patients can get along without your services for a while until you return. Notify them well in advance that you are closing the office for a specific period of time.

Other things to think about to prepare you and your business while you are away:

- Document your work flow and processes for those who will be supporting you during your break.
- When possible, take care of unfinished business issues.
- Prepare backup for anything that may come along, such as new business.
- Keep up liability and other insurance.
- Let everyone know important contact information, including accountants, lawyers, technical support, building maintenance, etc.
- Communicate in advance to all of your customers and clients about your plan and back-up plan so they know what to expect and whom to call.

Betsy, a hand surgeon in North Carolina, took a one-year break from her medical practice to volunteer in one of the poorest parts of South Africa. At first she doubted that she could leave her solo practice, but with her two employees leaving and a necessary move out of her medical building, she felt the time was right. She arranged for a new orthopedic doctor just moving to town to handle her patients for several months and was able to take the sabbatical of her dreams.

Though she was in single practice, she was still part of a larger, twenty-three-physician corporation. They had to vote to keep her in the corporation. She said that she still would have gone on sabbatical even if they said no. They didn't, but some believed she would not return.

Others in the local medical community were interested and positive. After she sent out letters to the larger medical community announcing her sabbatical, she was surprised to hear back from several doctors saying what a novel idea a sabbatical was in medicine and that they were envious. Her patients were very supportive and believed that she was coming back, which she did, and today she still has a thriving practice.

Glenn, an independent financial planner, worried that his clients would be unhappy when he told them about his plan to take three months off. Instead, they were impressed by his commitment and applauded his decision. Some even admitted they were jealous. His careful planning for covering their interests in his absence—offering to transfer accounts to another financial planner—was thorough and much appreciated. When he returned, some clients told him he was a role model and inspiration for them. Glenn's practice flourishes today.

PLANNING TRAVEL

Most people we interviewed included some form of travel as part of their sabbatical experience. Once you have identified where you want to go, you will need to research what is needed to enter the countries you would like to visit. Some have special visa requirements that might take from a week to three months to be processed. Although some people prefer to just head to a place and see what happens and make plans as they go, other types of travel require more advance planning. Reservations for travel, housing, rail, etc. might need to be made in advance. More importantly, make sure your passport is not only up to date, but will not expire within six months of entering any country.

For those looking to study while they are away, there is usually an application process with deadlines for enrollment. Researching everything you can and speaking to people who have done what you are planning to do will save time and aggravation and make the travel experience richer and more fulfilling. Plan early and ahead, when you can.

The Appendix includes a long and thorough list of things to consider and plan for before traveling as part of your Reboot Break, and Chapter 4 is also rich in travel planning information.

PLANNING TO VOLUNTEER

A desire to "give back" drives people to volunteer, and it may you as well. Volunteering can be part of a company's sabbatical program or sponsored by a church or community group. Other times it is part of the "new volunteerism," where you pay to volunteer in interesting places overseas or at home.

When Larry Fish accepted his job as Chairman and CEO of Citizens Financial Group in 1991, his predecessor said he could come on board whenever he liked. He decided to take a six-month sabbatical before he started. "I went to a social services housing agency and said, 'Look, I would like to help, but I don't want to do a strategic plan or raise money or fix the accounting department. I will scrub floors, mentor kids, work the food bank, and be here as early and late as you want.'"

So that's what he did, literally, for six months. "I got much more out of it than I gave," Fish said, "And I took the experience and started the sabbatical program at my institution." Citizens offers its full-time employees who have been with the bank for at least three years and are in good standing the opportunity to volunteer at a non-profit of their choice. They get full pay and benefits and a guarantee that the same job or better will be available when they return.

Other firms encourage volunteerism as well. Antonia talked of the experience of Shearman & Sterling LLP, a major New York law firm, giving its employees two to three months off to volunteer. "It makes us a better firm and makes us better lawyers as well as people."

Two organizations that list opportunities for volunteering abroad are Working Abroad and Greenforce. Working Abroad provides a scheduled report on volunteer activities across the world for a small fee. Greenforce, a London-based organization, runs volunteer programs in ten countries. Other resources are listed in the Appendix. Confirm that the organization is a registered 501(c)(3) at *www.guidestar.org*.

Before you sign on with a volunteer program, research the operator, the prices, and the environment. Some tour operators charge for organizing trips that you could do for free directly with the not-for-profit.

THE PLAN OUTLINE

The task now is to take the elements of your Reboot Break and plan step by step for each part. At this point, you know your goals and timeframe, have consulted with important people, including your boss and/or colleagues, and can now look into the details of what you will do on this well-deserved break. This is the fun part because it brings you closer to the reality of your coming adventure.

PLANNING GRID FOR A SUCCESSFUL REBOOT BREAK

Use the grid on the next page or make your own as a way to organize your thinking around each goal you want to achieve during your Reboot Break. First think about the bigger goals, i.e., improve your health, travel, spend time with the family, learn something new. As you drill down in any one of those larger sabbatical dreams, you will need to think through the various steps to make them happen. With each goal in mind, what will you need to do first? Build from there. Add who can help you realize your goals and by when.

Be as detailed and specific as possible, giving yourself timelines to ensure that you actually get it done. You can continue to add to the grid and change things as you learn from each step you take.

· SAMPLE PLANNING GRID ·				
Goals	Action Steps	Who Can Help	Timeframe for Action	Done
1. Save enough money to feel comfortable during the time off	Set up a Reboot Break. fund to cover living costs	Speak to financial advisor and make a plan	By the end of the month	
2. Study Spanish in a foreign country	Research what countries offer Spanish courses, and related costs	Find websites and people who have done this to determine the best place to go	Decide at least three months before I plan to leave	
3. Rent out my house or swap with someone else in Latin America or Spain for two months	Research the various options and determine which direction to take	Speak to someone who has swapped his/her house to understand the pros and cons	Decide six months before so I can get the house ready	

In the Appendix of this book is a simple planning checklist, plus more detailed planning tips, organized by timeframe starting at one year out. The steps can be compressed into a shorter timeframe as necessary, and not all steps apply to everyone.

READY FOR TAKEOFF

Having a solid plan and taking steps day-by-day toward the sabbatical dream will calm the jitters and keep the path clear for takeoff. Keeping your goals in mind, you can explore ideas and make choices. If your plan isn't working, that's okay, because you can always change it.

You are now armed with some of the tools and steps that can lead to a successful Reboot Break. It is the planning that makes it so. Look within yourself for what you really want to do and think through what it will take to get there. Everyone needs a break; you wouldn't be reading this book if you didn't think you needed one too. Planning is important, it can actually be fun, and it will lead to a more satisfying and successful Reboot Break.

▶ EXERCISES

Exercise 3-1: Building Your Dream Reboot Break

- Make a list of all the things you would ideally like to do while on your Reboot Break. Don't leave anything out; this is the time to throw in everything you have always thought about doing but never had the time to do.
- Now go through and prioritize the top 5, top 10, and top 15 things you would like to do.

Exercise 3-2: Taking Your "Business Case" to Your Employer

- Draft a sabbatical plan "business case" to take to your employer, including responses to questions the employer might ask and a list of the ways your time off would benefit the company or organization.

Exercise 3-3: Create Your Own Planning Checklist

- Review the Reboot Break Planning Checklist from the Appendix and the list of things to do when preparing ahead of time.
- Compile a list of what you need to get done and when before starting your Reboot Break, with timeframes to keep you on track.

CHAPTER 4

Funding Your Freedom

"Good fortune is what happens when
opportunity meets with planning."

—*Thomas Edison*

O ne of the greatest challenges people face in taking time
off is how to finance it. Maybe you're concerned about the current
economy. Maybe the market crash has sucked your retirement funds
dry. Maybe you are afraid to leave a job for fear of not finding another.
Or maybe you are already on an "unexpected sabbatical" because you
have lost your job. Maybe you fear that tapping into your savings will
leave you vulnerable or that you need the health insurance that your
employer provides. Or maybe you fear criticism from your family for
being "frivolous" with hard-earned money. In this chapter, we offer
creative ways of funding your freedom without putting your financial
health at risk.

Finding the money to buy your freedom and nourish your soul is
often the single biggest roadblock to getting away. Your goal should
be time off free of financial concerns so that you can focus on new
learning and experiences. That means, ideally, untouched retirement
funds and stable home finances.

Marco, who took two course-correction Reboot Breaks in his twenties (Chapter 2), put it well: "Financial worries—fear of financial insecurity, uncertainty, and instability—threaten one's identity. People have a fear of being in limbo, especially financial limbo. It takes an inner strength to set that period of uncertainty in place."

In this chapter, we'll show you:

- How to separate the misconceptions about financing Reboot Breaks from the reality.
- How to save for time off.
- How to plan your finances, including anticipating unexpected expenses and special considerations for the period when you are returning to work.
- Resources you may be able to draw on to help finance your break.

CLEARING UP THE MISCONCEPTIONS

You hear many misconceptions about funding and the ability to take time off from work, such as:

- Sabbaticals are only for middle- and upper-income people.
- A Reboot Break will bankrupt your savings.
- Taking time off will ruin your career.
- It's irresponsible to take a sabbatical, especially in bad economic times.

You don't have to be rich to take time off. We interviewed people from every income group who have taken time off. How much money someone makes is not the best predictor of who takes a sabbatical. It has more to do with the stage of life people are in and their dreams and goals. Teachers, nurses, ministers, construction workers, and other individuals have found ways to take a Reboot Break.

Three age groups tend to be the most interested in taking sabbaticals, and they fund them in different ways. The twenty- to thirty-year-olds we interviewed were able to pack up their apartments and leave stuff with their parents, if they had anything, and be free to take off on little money. The thirty- to fifty-year-olds had mortgages and other expenses, but were most likely to get some support from their employers or their own savings or find work while off work. The sixty-plus-year-olds tended to use savings for their time off.

One of the most important misconceptions is about the costs associated with taking time off. Yes, it does cost something to do what you'd like on sabbatical, but it doesn't have to break the bank.

People fund their time off using their retirement, vacation, education or travel funds, or funds from an account created specifically for a Reboot Break. We call this the "Reboot Break account," and it is an important vehicle for realizing your dreams. You can direct your own savings, as well as gifts from others, to help fund your time off in the future.

Some may use full or partial pay from a company sabbatical program (if there is one) and/or accumulated vacation time. Others tap severance packages, bonuses, family gifts, inheritances, or tax returns to fund their freedom. There are many financial possibilities and ways to begin imagining how you might finance your break.

Financial Impact on Your Career?

One of the most common fears we heard from people of all ages centered on the impact taking time off would have on their career. Many worried they would not be taken seriously or would be passed over for promotions and bonuses and thus suffer financial consequences. They wondered how to explain the employment gap in the future.

Some were concerned about colleagues who were competitive with them, and what they might do to take over their positions. In a shaky economy, where people have seen much of their gains in the stock market evaporate, their companies downsize, and their neighbors out of work, there is an understandable reluctance to do something risky. Some were concerned that their jobs would not be there when they returned.

We found you do not have to sacrifice your career and financial stability to take time off. Of the 200 people we interviewed, over half went back to their current employers, and every one of them ended up feeling that they were more valued by their company. Those who didn't go back or severed the relationship before going on sabbatical ended up in positions they liked as well. It turns out that career breaks can be good for your financial as well as your personal life.

Over 60 percent of Generation X employees, born between 1964 and 1978, want to take an extended leave or sabbatical, according to a 2001 survey quoted by *American Demographics*. Many progressive employers see it as a sign of drive and initiative. Travel abroad builds interpersonal and cultural skills. Our interviewees learned new languages, talents, and work-related knowledge on their time off. Being in new cultures made them more flexible, adaptable, and tolerant.

Many people prepared for their return before taking off by doing speeches before and during the sabbatical, going to industry conferences, staying current on the literature of their industry, and checking with recruiters on how they would be perceived on their return, even going so far as to revise their resumes to explain the time off before they left, and sending them out a month or two before their return.

The Connection Between Money and Sabbatical Goals

Research by psychologists and economists indicates that people see money as a source of security, freedom, prestige, power, and reward.

Taking time off is viewed as a source of freedom—the freedom to do what you want, enjoy a more balanced life and still feel secure about your future and that of your family. The burden of making a living often keeps us from stepping back and re-evaluating our lives. A Reboot Break allows us that time.

Interestingly, sometimes the wealthier people are, the more they fear taking time off because they are so tied to a certain level of income and spending. The thought of breaking the tie between money and happiness, or at least questioning it through a sabbatical, is too frightening. All of us at one time or another *need* time out to question our beliefs. We talk more about how to define success beyond money in Chapter 10, Living the Lifelong Sabbatical.

No one can predict what will happen with the economy or financial markets for the next few years. All of us have been impacted by living through the dramatic changes in home values, retirement accounts, and jobs in this economic downturn. But you can be proactive and take steps to get your finances under control. Hard-earned savings can go quickly if thought isn't given to what you want to do and how to do it.

Living Light

One new notion includes the concept of "living light"—saving as much as you can, spending wisely, and letting go of material things in exchange for more true freedom. Let's walk through what this means.

Leena, whose story you first read in Chapter 2, had a beautiful home in London but gave it up when she decided to take time off. "I had to let go of certain attachments. I had an exquisite flat in London. I decorated it but only lived there for three years. In order to take time off, I had to rent it out. My friends were horrified that I would leave this place I had just designed and furnished. **By letting go of material attachments, though, I was able to have my freedom.**"

For decades, America has been a "more is better" society: more food, more fashion, more money, and more spending. The global financial crisis has curbed our profligate tendencies and struck fear in consumers' hearts. With housing values plummeting and 401(k)s shrinking, saving for tomorrow makes sense.

More Americans today are "living light"—lightening up on debt, forgoing excessive spending, and spurning showy, expensive brands. This is not only necessary for most; it's also appealing. More and more, we are looking beyond conspicuous consumption to find meaning in life's more prosaic pleasures, such as spending time with family and friends.[1]

---

1 "The New Consumer Value: 'Living Light.'" *www.santa-fe-group.com/wp-content/ uploads/2010/07/NewConsumerValueNov2008.pdf*

Living light is a fundamental of a Reboot Break. Few of us can afford to maintain an extravagant lifestyle while we're working, never mind while taking time off from work. Instead, many sabbatical takers free themselves in the same way Leena did: by forgoing material possessions in exchange for more authentic personal fulfillment.

Kevin, like many others we interviewed, learned to live on less and to become much less attached to material things. He found ways to travel more inexpensively and live more authentically. He consciously chose on his Reboot Breaks to find ways to simplify his life to give him the breathing room to think.

CASH OUT YOUR RETIREMENT SAVINGS, HOME, OR BUSINESS?

A sabbatical is meant to give you time away from work to refresh, renew, reflect, and then come back to your same employer or business or decide to do something else. Cashing in your retirement fund or selling your home or business may put undue financial or emotional pressures on you. If you're thinking of doing this, be sure you've given yourself time to think seriously about what you want to do next. You may be surprised that after your time off, you wish you had kept the house or business, and certainly want the security of your retirement savings. Few people taking a career break cash in everything and take off. Keeping a tie to your home, work, non-profit board, or family is important. Having a place to come back to at the end of the journey may be critical to your happiness on your Reboot Break.

CREATING A BUDGET

Nothing works better than creating and adhering to a budget when you need to plan or when money is tight. While some people think of budgets as a chore, they are powerful tools for realizing goals. So start with your goals and include the amount of time off you want to give yourself before you go back to work. Your career break may be voluntary or not, but in tough economic times, we all worry. Having a structure for your budget is critical to using this time between jobs or careers. The basics of budgeting for a sabbatical include:

- Determining your current spending needs and cash flow.
- Determining the approximate amount of time you want to take off.
- Listing the bills that will need to be paid, such as mortgage, insurance, college tuition, etc., on an ongoing basis.
- Determining specific financial needs while on sabbatical, such as travel funds.
- Brainstorming ways to cut costs or earn money, such as renting your home or apartment during your period away.

To understand how you spend money, plot out the previous year's monthly expenditures. Include tax statements, credit card statements, check registers, and other documentation you have on hand. If you don't have all these records, get financial planning software, such as a spreadsheet, or get a notebook and record all expenditures each day, week, and month for a few months. Include credit purchases, as well as cash, debit, and direct payments. Use a spreadsheet or notebook or online software to create categories going forward for revenue and expenses. Start tracking now in preparation for your time off as well as during the sabbatical. Just the process of writing things down or recording them daily is enlightening.

You will begin to see ways to save automatically. We tend to spend more freely with credit cards, and often don't realize how much we spend on snacks, coffee, and other things we really don't need. Identify areas of spending where you can cut back before and during your time off—from gym fees to gifts—as well as those expenditures that remain constant, such as the mortgage or car payments.

When Rita started planning for her most recent leave from work, she started keeping track of daily expenses and income to help understand better how to budget. "I was shocked at how much I was spending daily on frivolous things. By recording them, I knew just where to cut back without much pain." She continues to monitor her spending in this way today.

Next, draw up a monthly budget that allows for realizing your financial goals: saving for a sabbatical, spending on sabbatical, paying down all credit cards, saving money for a down payment on a house, putting money into the retirement fund, etc. Microsoft Money and Quicken have excellent budgeting and cash flow planning forms. Or search online for other budgeting software. (In the Appendix is a listing of some resources to help you develop and track a budget.) The budget process should include not only what income you have to draw on and expenses you can cut, but also other resources you can tap in an emergency. These might be savings, loans, rental income, or sale of a major asset.

In addition to being one of the most rewarding experiences in your life, taking a Reboot Break may also teach you financial planning skills and practices. The process of planning, saving, budgeting, and controlling spending before and during the time you take off will serve you the rest of your life. An added benefit may be learning that you can take risks and succeed.

WAYS TO FUND YOUR FREEDOM

Let's start with some of the ways you might fund your freedom, categorized into four types:

- Saving ahead of time
- Getting your employer to pay
- Getting paid for work done while on sabbatical
- Using a windfall

SAVING AHEAD OF TIME

The more you save ahead of time, the more stress-free your time off will be and the more options you will have. Using "found money," like a severance or inheritance or a large tax return, can be the initial basis for that savings, as can be regular contributions to a "Reboot Break account." Saving is a commitment to yourself and to your goals. Putting even small sums away each week or month creates momentum.

Ways to Save:

- **Automating savings from your paycheck** through direct deposit with your employer or via your bank. You pay your Reboot Break account first and adjust your spending accordingly. Once you start, you may find it's not as hard as you think, so review the amount you're saving every few months and consider saving even more.
- **Asking your friends and relations to contribute** to a Reboot Break account in lieu of giving you holiday, birthday, and other types of gifts.
- **Earning more** through a raise, bonus, overtime, extra job, or investment and putting those extra earnings into your Reboot Break account. This allows you to continue with your current spending habits while you build a reserve for the time off.
- **Renting out your home or apartment,** your office space, your second home, or anything else that might be of value to others in order to offset your living expenses.
- **"Cashing out" or liquidating any assets** you no longer want or need. Use eBay, consignment shops, garage sales, auctions, and other venues and reserve the returns for your time off.
- **Putting your money out of easy reach** of your ATM card, debit card, or checkbook. Make it a savings account, CD, or other account where it is out of mind and less accessible.
- **Changing jobs or building your business** to give yourself more earning power, and then saving the difference for your break.
- **Asking your employer to defer your income or pay 75 percent of your salary now and the rest when you are "rebooting your life."** Learning to live on less before the sabbatical is good practice for living light.
- **Managing your credit cards** by trying to pay off your balances each month, which will save you interest and fees.

While you are contributing to the Reboot Break account, don't forget to max out (contribute as much as is possible to) any 401(k)s, especially if they are matched by your employer. Many employers will match what you put into savings anywhere from 50 percent to 100 percent. You are leaving money on the table if you do not continue to fund any matching program your employer has while you are taking time off. If you are over fifty, you can contribute more than the stipulated $15,000 as a way of catching up, and it is prudent to do so. The 401(k) savings will continue to grow your retirement and back-up "emergency fund" as you take time off from your career.

Build a safety net or "emergency fund" by putting money into savings, like a high-yield money market fund or laddered short-term CD, with at least six months income to cover monthly expenses. This is your safety net to be used and replenished for emergencies, such as car breakdowns, repairs to the house, to cover unexpected loss of income, or if it takes you longer to find a position when you return from your between-gigs sabbatical. Always replenish it.

Some other advice, depending on your age and financial situation, that helps in planning your finances for a sabbatical:

- Save at least 15 to 20 percent of your income for long-term goals, such as owning a house, college tuition, and retirement.
- Keep your debt-to-income ratio at no more than 30 percent.
- Look at refinancing when rates are at least one percentage point lower than your existing rate.
- Invest no more that 5 percent of your stock portfolio in your company stock, or any single stock.
- Keep discretionary spending under 20 percent of your take-home pay.
- Keep your FICO/credit score high.

Saving for time off gives you the freedom to do what you want without having to tap family resources or worry how you will impact your finances. Bruce, who worked for a financial analysis division of a large institution, spent several years planning for his time off, budgeting for expenses, living on his salary alone, and banking his bonuses in a savings account. His good saving habits allowed him to take an entire year off.

Rita consciously chose to leave her position as President of Mead-Westvaco's Consumer Division to take time off, then start a "portfolio career." She worked with her financial advisor ahead of time to plan for the transition. She prepaid many expenses, including her mortgage, used stock options for savings, maximized her deferred income while she was working, and chose to live a more simple lifestyle after leaving her full-time job.

What If I Haven't Saved for My Sabbatical?

If you need time off now and haven't saved enough, the next best thing is to "borrow" from your existing savings. Your home equity line of credit (HELOC) is a good place to start, as interest on a loan up to $100,000 is tax deductible, usually at a reasonable rate. However, HELOCs are harder to get if the value of your home has gone down. (The average American home lost 13 percent to 20 percent of its value between 2005 and 2009.) The ratio of equity required has gone up as well. Shop *www.bankrate.com* for example rates for home equity lines of credit. While we don't advocate taking money early from your 401(k) or any account that might carry a penalty for withdrawal, some people have done just that with a plan to replenish the account.

Borrow only when it makes good financial sense for you. By 2007, US households owed $1.33 for every $1 of disposable income. Look at your debt-to-income ratio (monthly debt payments divided by monthly pre-tax income) and stay under 30 percent.

Here are some questions to ask when considering borrowing to finance your break:

- Are you investing in yourself/your career to enhance your value as an employee or entrepreneur, and ultimately add to your net worth?

- Is your credit score high enough to qualify for the lowest rates?
- Will you be able to afford the payments if you're out of work for six months?
- Will your debt repayments remain under 30 percent of your pre-tax monthly income when you return to work?

When your preparation timeline is short, there are still some things you can do to set the stage for time off. First, try to pay down your credit card debts as much as possible. Transfer credit card balances to lower-interest cards or call your issuer to lower the interest rate. (Call your credit card companies to negotiate, since more than half of them will reduce interest rates when a customer calls and makes the request.) If you can, pay off the cards with higher interest first, then the next higher. Mortgage and home equity debt (up to $100,000), however, are tax deductible. If your interest rate is low, you're better off paying the minimum amount due and paying out over time. Payments on student loans are also tax deductible, so pay them off last.

To get the best credit terms, you need high credit scores. The best rates go to those with scores of 760 or higher out of a possible 850. Boost your score by paying bills on time, reducing credit card balances to less than 20 percent of your limits, and correcting any errors on your reports. Order your credit report from *www.annualcreditreport .com*. You get one free from each credit bureau every twelve months. Buy the Equifax version of your FICO scores for $8 at their website.

The factors lenders look at in a credit report are:

1. How many inquiries you have made. (It's better to shop for loans in a fourteen-day window to have them recorded as only one.)
2. What you are juggling. (Having a mix of types of credit is considered an indicator of credit-worthiness.)
3. How much credit you are using. (Aim to use less than 20 percent.)
4. How timely you've been in paying bills: thirty to sixty days is yellow, which means they have the account on watch, and over ninety is red, which means in arrears and will impact your rating.

5. Whether you've ever really messed up: foreclosures, bankruptcies, liens, and other major problems will stay on your report for seven to ten years.

Some people borrow from family members or their regular savings. Most said they hoped to repay the amounts in the future, either to the family member they borrowed from, or to their savings. But many borrowed from their savings without worrying about paying it back right away because they understood the importance of the time off and that, regardless of finances, they had made an excellent return on their investment—their investment in themselves.

GETTING YOUR EMPLOYER TO PAY

Looking to cut costs without laying off employees in 2009, the New York law firm Skadden, Arps, Slate, Meagher & Flom LLP began offering associates worldwide the option of accepting one-third of their base salary to take a year off, especially to volunteer and do pro bono work. As part of the offer, they were guaranteed job security: if there were layoffs while they were away, Skadden assured them, they would be immune.

Also as a cost-cutting measure, KPMG has offered employees paid sabbaticals at 20 percent of their salaries, keeping their benefits intact and guaranteeing their jobs upon their return.

Academic sabbaticals are the norm because colleges and universities recognize that professors need to be refreshed and renewed periodically, in order to return to the classroom excited and invigorated. Academics are paid during their time off by the university or college for research or teaching in another area, geographically or intellectually.

To apply for a sabbatical, academics are usually required to have taught at the institution for at least seven years. In their applications, instructors set out a plan for what they will do and usually make a presentation to the faculty upon their return. The time off may be a semester, half year, or year.

Increasingly, nonacademic organizations, such as corporations, churches, non-profits, and legal and consulting firms, are providing financial support of some type for their employees to take time off to renew as well, as described in Chapters 1 and 3. We offer several examples of the types of programs and the benefits to the organization.

If you plan to stay with the same employer, the ideal situation is to convince them to pay you your salary while you are taking the sabbatical, or work out a special deal. Geoff told us about a creative approach someone took of getting his employer to pay half his salary for six months and defer the income to the next year. Then he took the next year off at 70–80 percent salary, so that he had income all along and tax advantages as well. This is just another example of deferred income that many highly paid executives use. You have the organization spread out your salary over a longer period of time, especially into years where you might not have as much income normally.

When planning for a break where you expect to return to the same company, it is important to negotiate explicitly that the time off is for "retooling" or "renewal" that will benefit the company and should contribute toward service, options, restricted stock, 401(k) matching eligibility, prior years' service, long-term disability, etc. Ask your employer how they will consider the time off in terms of vesting for retirement or stock options. We recommend negotiating with your employer for continued health insurance coverage paid by them, paying it yourself by reimbursing your employer, or finding some interim coverage. Even though health insurance can be expensive, you don't want to have it as a worry when you are taking time off.

Explore with your human resources department the option of going back to school for undergraduate or graduate work and/or coursework that would help you in your career. Often corporations will reimburse all or part of employee tuition costs. While this isn't exactly your employers paying for a sabbatical, it does pay for your education and expenses related to it when on your break. There are many programs that go unused because employees do not know of them.

Getting Paid While Taking Time Off

We found many creative ways people made money while on sabbatical by being inventive as well as persuasive. Here are some examples:

- **Rent your house,** office space, second home, or other real estate so you will have income coming in despite your taking time off.
- **Freelance your skills** in other environments—graphic design, teaching, doing artwork, babysitting, doing bookkeeping, cutting hair, travel writing—all while you are on sabbatical.
- **Apply for a grant or fellowship,** as there are many in the arts, writing, government service, and corporate world that are underutilized. It takes some digging, but they are there.
- **Apply for an internship** and learn a new field of work, industry, or set of skills. Many pay a small stipend or offer other benefits.
- **Be a travel companion** and learn about compassion as well as a different perspective on travel.
- **Explore opportunities to give lectures abroad** and represent your country, company, or industry. At least the expenses may be covered.
- **Try out a passion by getting another job,** such as being a sous chef or getting part-time work in a field you want to enter. (Get a job that is not too demanding so that you can do other things.)
- **Write your own blog** or articles for travel magazines, special interest magazines, or other publishers. Get a sponsor for your blog.
- **Start a business that you can do minimally from home or while traveling.** Internet-based businesses are more amenable to this.

Remember, Cathy and her husband paid for much of their eleven-month journey through Asia by lecturing for the U.S. Information Agency (USIA) on how Congress works and how to market to the United States. USIA paid for hotels, meals, transportation, and a small per diem when they were giving lectures sponsored by embassies, academic institutions, or newspapers. "It was a fabulous experience and paid for much of our time in those countries."

Rick, a potter, found a two-month visiting artist program at Arizona State University, which allowed him to explore new techniques and types of clay work. While it did not provide a stipend, it did provide housing, a place to work, and access to resources at the university.

Jan used a National Endowment for the Arts fellowship to return to university for a master's program and upgrade her skill set. She had been a reporter before and returned to the journalism field after her sabbatical, this time as a newscaster. Her time off not only gave her new skills, but the confidence to be front and center with her audience.

The caveat, however, is not to get so focused on making money that you defeat the purpose of taking time off. While working, albeit differently, during a sabbatical may ease your financial concerns, it may also deter you from the reflection and breaking away time you need. Disconnecting from work is one of the most important things to do, our interviewees say. That's what allows you to get perspective. If you work during your time off, be sure to put enough boundaries around it to leave yourself free time. Make the work fit into your overall goal, rather than the other way around.

Using a Windfall

Some of the people we interviewed used windfalls that came their way to pay for their time off. They ranged from inheritances to severance payments to bonuses and large tax refunds. Sometimes they were annual gifts from family members.

Unemployment Benefits

Unemployment benefits can be used to fund sabbaticals too. Amy, an attorney who was let go from her law firm because of the collapse of the corporate litigation department, used her unemployment check while doing an internship at a winemaking organization. The unemployment benefit allowed her to do the internship for no pay and was granted by the state because she was improving her chances for a new position.

CUTTING BACK ON EXPENSES

Looking closely at all your current spending patterns can help you find ways to cut costs and reallocate spending while on your Reboot Break. It's a matter of being open to changing your patterns of spending and saving. Acknowledge that there is flexibility in your budget, and you are off on the right foot! All of us have had to do this, but most of us only do so when forced.

Your sabbatical need not be an expensive proposition. Being flexible in what you want to do and how you do it takes more of the pressure off. As Bruce, whom you met earlier in this chapter, said, "Think about your expenses realistically and make sure you are comfortable so that stress about money does not interfere with your plan. Have good control over your expenses."

If you plan to travel for all or most of the time, think about what you won't need to spend money on during that time period: your home or apartment, your car, your office space, cable TV, housekeeper, car insurance, dry cleaners, gym membership, etc. Cancel or re-negotiate memberships until you return from your break. Try for a zero cost, or at least costs at one-third to one-half of normal living. One interviewee had great advice for the sabbatical period: "Just stay out of the stores!"

Cut Your Home Expenses

Cutting your home expenses while you're taking a Reboot Break can turn it into independent bliss. Sabbatical costs are, and should be, different from everyday life costs. Be inventive, imaginative, and thoughtful in what you do. Your savings will deplete quickly if your ongoing home expenses continue at the current level.

Before you take time off, prepay expenses such as taxes, insurance, contributions to retirement plans, and fees that may come up while you are off work. Do your regular medical and dental checkups before you leave employment. Ask a friend or your accountant or financial advisor to pay bills while you are gone, and give them power of attorney for any emergencies that come up. Housing costs and maintenance are often the largest expenditures per month. Some ways to cut housing costs are:

- **Renting your apartment or home** at a rate that covers mortgage and utilities payments. Ideally, rent it furnished to save on storage and moving costs. Use a rental agent or do it yourself, but get references and credit checks and write out a contract for the renters, even if they are friends or family.
- **Getting a house sitter** who can watch the house, take care of pets, pay bills, take care of repairs, etc. while you are away. Create a contract for this, to make the house sitter more like a professional. This eliminates the cost of paying someone to do these things for you.
- **Trading or swapping your apartment or home** through an Internet business, such as *www.homeexchange.com*, or a network of your friends who have houses in desirable places. This at least mitigates the costs of a new place.
- **Selling your home,** but only if you are looking to buy elsewhere or that is part of your sabbatical plan. There are costs to doing this, and the market should be right.

We'll expand on the concept of trading your house or apartment, because it is becoming a major trend and many opportunities are emerging. Are you planning to travel to a foreign country? Do you want to have some time to write your great American novel, but do it on the coast of California?

Many people interested in living in a different area for a period of time are looking to trade or rent houses and apartments for that short period. There are websites that vet potential candidates for you and provide you with choices of homes and apartments elsewhere. Some of those sites are listed in the Appendix.

There are also listings at universities and colleges, where professors who take sabbaticals look for short-term rentals. If you live in the New York or Washington DC areas, there are diplomats who are always looking for short-term rentals or stays. The same goes for cities all over the world where there are large diplomatic communities.

Talk to your accountant or financial advisor about possible tax implications of what you are doing, from renting your house to what can be deducted for education or career enhancement. Even if you don't earn money during your time off, if it results in the publication of a book or research for a project, there may be tax relief opportunities.

If the sabbatical involves a legitimate professional activity, everything (within limits, of course) may be deductible as a business expense if you leave your home. In case you're ever audited, keep excellent records so that you'll be able to demonstrate how the expenses contributed to your business or career enhancement. If you stay away for a year or more, up to $80,000 in foreign income can be excluded from your federal income taxes. Renting your house and any repairs that are made while it's being rented are tax deductible, too. Talk to your tax advisor!

Budget Travel

While some of you may be accustomed to staying at nice hotels and eating at good restaurants as part of your business or regular life, traveling on a budget during your time off can open you to the real life and culture of a country.

When Cathy and Gary traveled in Asia for a year in 1985, they tried to live on $50 a day. "We often did so by saving on transport," Cathy says, "and that is where we really had some fabulous experiences, such as riding from Karachi to Peshawar, Pakistan in a brightly colored, patterned bus with people, poultry, and potatoes. Another was riding on a junk around Hong Kong with a Chinese family, rather than taking the tour boat. We visited the outer islands of Japan by traveling on a mail boat. In all cases, they were safe modes of transportation and quite clean . . . but not the expected way for tourists to travel. A highlight was traveling through the jungles of Thailand on an elephant, by boat, and on foot."

The point is, open your mind to new adventures on your Reboot Break!

Housing can include hostels, bed-and-breakfasts, guest houses, or a friend's apartment. For those more outdoor-oriented, there is camping or caravan hires. And then there's always the overnight train that combines transport with housing. The real treat of staying in places like these is the people you meet, and it is those people and experiences you tend to remember, not the fifteenth Hilton hotel room you've stayed in.

Another advantage of budget travel is that you spend more time walking, exploring free sites, just "being" rather than spending money on shows, events, paid museums, etc. You have more time for reading, writing, hiking, and reflection. Don't exchange busyness at work for busyness in travel.

One way Cathy saved money on her sabbatical in 2007 was to trade her house in Santa Fe for a house in Dordogna, France, owned by a friend. Both were big enough houses to accommodate friends or family for three weeks, and the costs were minimal—cleaning people, tips for the overseers, and utilities. It gave Cathy and her friends three weeks in France for the cost of getting there. Saving on eating out by cooking in breakfasts and some dinners was a plus. In fact, they would have missed out on the fabulous food markets had they stayed in a hotel. She still dreams about the good breads and pure butter from the markets. The fact that both houses were comfortable, attractive, and located in key tourist areas was fundamental to the reason for choosing those places for travel centers.

David, an entrepreneur who lost his business and was in mourning for the time and effort down the drain, took off for Prague, where it was less expensive to live. "I lived for four months on $1,000. I had saved some money, rented my apartment, and scaled way back financially. It was one of the most interesting times of my life. I learned things I could never have learned the way I lived before. Being free of the 'material stuff' allowed me to explore what life had to offer."

One way to travel free is to save up your frequent flier miles and use them for travel during the sabbatical. Use credit cards that help you to earn points, and try to concentrate them on one or two airlines.

Other considerations include how long you want to be gone and whether you are willing to rent or trade your home. Do you need rental income, or will a trade work for you? Who could look after your property while you are gone? Do you have a place to store valuables? What kind of a place are you looking for? What would you have to do to your house or apartment to make it attractive to trade?

At the very least, you need to give someone the responsibility for looking after your home or apartment, paying bills, picking up mail, and having power of attorney for emergencies. You can automate many financial payments through direct deposit and bill payment with your bank or through a bill payment service.

Other Ways to Save Money

Get your family in on the planning on ways to save money. A 2009 *USA Today* survey on the economic downturn showed that 74 percent of children were worried about, and 67 percent wanted to talk to their parents about, the family finances.

Beth, a vice president of a major manufacturing firm in New York, enlisted her husband and children in the planning a year ahead of their family sabbatical. They took a year off, home-schooled their four kids, and traveled all over the United States in a retrofitted bus with a car towed behind. They tapped in to savings and sold some stock options to fund the year off. The kids were told they would have no spending money unless they earned it themselves. Each was told to create a job or find ways to raise money. At the time, they were two, six, nine, and eleven. The three older kids got into it and had jobs, such as pet sitting and lawn care, to raise their spending money for the year they took off. The whole family went through things to sell and had a huge garage sale, plus cleaned up their house! Everyone agreed not to buy new clothes for the year except at secondhand stores. They agreed not to order but one drink at restaurants and to eat healthy snacks along the route. While they had originally planned to sell their house, they decided to rent it and were glad they had it to come back to at the end of the sabbatical.

You don't have to travel far or spend much money at all to enjoy your time off. Many of the people we interviewed treated their hometowns as places to explore and acted as if they were tourists in their area, visiting museums, shops, schools, theatres, farms, and other places on long weekends or daily jaunts. It's time to realize it has been years since you went to some of the places your houseguests love.

The Unexpected Sabbatical Survival Plan

If you have been let go by your employer, can you still fund time off without being worried about finances and finding another job when you return? The answer is yes, if you take a breath and think about it.

First, see what can be negotiated with your employer. Is there a severance package? Outplacement services? Continuation of benefits? Use of company facilities? Payment for attendance at conferences? Payment for financial planning?

Apply for unemployment benefits as soon as possible. While it is not in any way a replacement for your salary, it is something and will help you get through. Look at applying for social security or company pensions if you are over sixty. You may find it worthwhile to begin drawing them earlier.

Sit down with your family and go over what has happened and what resources you have. By making them part of the process, they will worry less and you will all face the challenges together. They can also be a resource for you to explore new job and career opportunities.

If you have never created a budget, now is the time to do so. Treat the unexpected sabbatical as you would a regular sabbatical. Look where expenses can be reduced and where assets you may have can be rented or traded or sold.

Take at least a couple of weeks to a month to do nothing but mourn the job loss, get yourself organized, and take time to reconnect with your family, your friends, your body, and your mind. Chances are it has been stressful leading up to the job loss, and you need the time to recoup mentally and physically before you start a job hunt.

Give yourself time even when you are in the job hunt process. Even those on an unexpected sabbatical found ways, after taking a month or two to reboot, to contain their job hunt to three or four days a week to give them downtime to think more strategically.

THIS CHAPTER IS just the beginning of thinking about funding your freedom . . . there are many stories and good ideas to come in the next few chapters. The Appendix has a list of resources and a sample financial planning list that will help you think through what you need to do. There are myriad ways to fund your time off and enjoy the insights that brings. View it as one of the best financial investments you will ever make!

▶ EXERCISES

Exercise 4-1: Facing Your Fears

- What are your biggest fears about money and taking time off from work? Write them down. Write potential solutions next to the fears.

Exercise 4-2: Figuring Out What You Need

- Write down how much money you think you will need to maintain your ongoing financial obligations and expenses during your Reboot Break.

- Write down potential sources of funds you might tap in to to finance your time off.
- What is the gap and how will you fill it?

(Note: the Appendix has a sample budget checklist.)

Exercise 4-3: Cutting Back on Expenses

- Write down ten ways you can cut back on expenses before and during your sabbatical.

CHAPTER 5

Phases and Navigating the First Thirty Days

"Go confidently in the directions of your dreams!
Live the life you've imagined.
As you simplify your life,
the laws of the universe will be simpler."

—Henry David Thoreau

Every Reboot Break is unique, but our interviews revealed a common pattern of how sabbatical takers allocated their time. Most tended to divide time into major blocks, each with a different quality and feel to it. Many people think about their break in quarters. The character and length of the phases vary, but in general they describe the rhythms you can expect during your time off. The next three chapters explore these four phases of a Reboot Break. This chapter introduces the phases and covers the first phase in more depth, especially the first thirty days.

PHASES OF A SABBATICAL

I. Creating Space—Putting your life in order
II. Reconnection—Revitalizing connections to people, places, activities, and self

III. Exploration—Learning new things, especially through travel

IV. Reentry—Starting a new chapter of your life

Phase I, the "Creating Space" stage, often involves sorting, cleaning, and simplifying one's environment. This is a time of regrouping, of clearing and "getting your house in order" so that the time spent can be as free and uncluttered as possible. Many people don't know what to do with themselves in the beginning. It's not uncommon to experience work withdrawal or contact withdrawal.

In particular, **the first thirty days are crucial—they set the stage for the rest of the time off**. They are also, for many, a shock to the system, going from a busy work life to time off.

Once the Creating Space period is done, sabbatical takers feel comfortable expanding their horizons. They tend toward activities in their town or city that they enjoyed but hadn't done for years. We call this stage "Reconnection." Reconnection is a time of reaching out to others and enjoying personal growth. During this period, people broaden their horizons by trying new things, renewing old connections, and rediscovering passions long left behind.

This is a time to explore new or old or forgotten activities—from new foods to taking a dance class to picking up a new sport. The adventure of Reconnection is often coupled with the comfort and fun of reaching out to friends and family, especially people sabbatical takers have not had time to see during their busy everyday lives. They are able to enjoy the little pleasures in life, like reading the newspaper cover to cover, cooking dinner for a friend, going to a play, taking a walk, or writing in a journal.

After a period of fun and revitalization, sabbatical takers are ready to test the waters with more adventure and greater risks, often farther from home. We call this stage "Exploration." Whether traveling to Asia, taking Spanish classes, exploring your spiritual side on a retreat to the American Southwest, or embarking on a volunteer project in Africa, external adventures can lead to internal journeys and explorations of the mind and self, giving birth to new and unexpected interests and passions.

After a time of Exploration, people are refreshed and exhilarated, and ready to consider their next gig. Reflecting on their experiences, ideally over a period of months, they are able to "reenter" and begin to shape a new stage in their personal and work lives. This fourth stage of the sabbatical, "Reentry," is where a new chapter of your life begins. This is one of the most exciting and satisfying parts of rebooting your life, as you assimilate what you have experienced and make time for reflection. It is a time of new ideas, new possibilities, and new perspectives.

While not everyone goes through the four stages in the same way, this last phase, Reentry, is one that should not be rushed. Too often, people try to predict what they will do at the end of the sabbatical before they've even started. We encourage readers not to feel pressure to answer when your families and colleagues ask what you're going to do at the end. The answer will come when it's time.

Time for reflection is so important at this stage because it is where the activities and experiences, the emotions and feelings, and the wants and needs come together to pave the path to post-reboot life. Reentry is usually about coming to terms with the end of a wonderful period in your life and figuring out how to incorporate all those wonderful experiences in the future, as you set about to return to work or to start a new profession.

The next three chapters describe how we and those we interviewed divided and navigated our time off. This chapter is dedicated to the first phase—the first thirty days and how to think about a daily schedule. The next chapter will segue into the Reconnection and Exploration stages, and Chapter 7, on Reentry, will address the process and potential fears of seeking that new career or returning to work when you're moving to a new chapter in your life.

THE FIRST THIRTY DAYS

One would think that the first day of a Reboot Break would be the happiest of one's life. No work, no worries, and a whole bunch of free time. What could be better?

For many, it is wonderful from the beginning, but others experience anxiety about the change. And don't be surprised if you even feel unwell in the early days. You might feel nauseated, have headaches, or find you can't eat. Some find that their bodies need to "detox" as the stress dissipates. As Lori shared:

I had a physical reaction. I was literally dizzy. My head was spinning from having operated at such a pace that my body had a hard time slowing down. All that adrenaline had no place to go. This was the most dramatic time. My euphoria was muted by confusion about my physical reaction.

Many report that they did not know what to do with themselves in the beginning. It's not uncommon to experience work withdrawal or contact withdrawal. Rita said: I found during my second break that I suffered from email withdrawal.

For me, email was like brushing my teeth; it was one of the first things I did each morning. After getting over 100 emails a day and needing to check email multiple times a day, it felt strange not having this ritual or habit in my daily life.

Others reported sleeping until noon. Fear was common, too. Susan said she woke up on the first Monday and was terrified. She was so used to being scheduled all her life. Jason felt guilty not going to work. Jerry also said that at first he had trouble not being in a routine. He told us, **"Starting a Reboot Break is a shock. It's a loss of rhythm, rhyme, and reason."**

Dr. Roberta Lee knows a lot about decompressing. As the Medical Director of Beth Israel's Continuum Center for Health and Healing in New York City, she has seen hundreds of people suffering from stress and burnout from work. She has written a book called *The SuperStress Solution* and is a frequent speaker on the topic of how to relieve stress in our lives. She believes that stress frequently implies that you have gotten out of touch with what is comfortable in work.

And she thinks Reboot Breaks are a great idea. "They afford time to immerse yourself, to step out of your work self, and to see the totality of how stress got you where you are. The first thirty days need to be a time of recovery. Each person has his or her own rhythm. Everyone goes through different phases; there is usually a period of regrouping, and a period of the body recovering and recouping."

Stress manifests itself in different ways. For some it's in stomach problems, while others have neck or back problems. And for others their immune systems are more vulnerable. Some people are much more affected by stress than others.

There is also a difference in how men and women handle stress. Often women in high-powered careers give up friendships. Tending and befriending can help them recover. A distinct pattern of recovery with women is the need to talk issues out. Some career women have become so masculine that they assume the way to reduce stress is by finding quiet time, when in reality they need relationships. Men, on the other hand, tend to seek quiet time, "cave time." But they need relationships too.

Dr. Lee believes the first thirty days offer an important time and space to ask yourself: Are you living well, and what helps or hinders you? How many friends and loved ones do you have around? How many have you pushed away? This is particularly an issue for men.

She recommends staying in touch with your dreams. Every life that sparkles is a much more stress-resilient life. It's good to have five- and ten-year goals and dreams.

Dr. Lee also recommends keeping a journal so that you can get in touch with parts of you that you have tended to ignore while you were in the highly focused part of your job. "There are lots of things going on in our heads that we don't even know about. Journaling is a great way to get in touch with the ticker tape in our head. If you have the option of a sabbatical, I would encourage you to do it. It's a way of valuing your life and yourself."

In addition to journaling, we recommend treating the first week or even month of your break as a time for indulgence. Get a massage. Read junk novels. Make a schedule and fill it with activities that you enjoy. Jason, who turned from art framing to massage therapy, spent the first month learning the natural rhythms of his body for sleeping and waking, which helped to clear his mind.

One UK couple chose to spend their time off mostly traveling. They spent the first three weeks of their first month in the United States "doing nothing" in a remote, secluded cabin. "It was fantastic," said Nigel. "We did a bit of skiing, a bit of walking, and chilled out. It was a nice, relaxing way to start our year off."

Victor found he needed two or three months to decompress. "Not having a preconceived time schedule is very smart. Letting go of all the tension from work is a great thing."

Beverly said, "I loved the joy of not having to be in any one place at a certain time."

Jerry agreed, adding, "There were fewer rules and less fitting in required. I didn't feel I had to be in places. I could sleep or exercise or not."

Ariane de Bonvoisin, reboot veteran and author of *The First 30 Days*, said:

> *The first thirty days can last 10 or 200 because it's related to the mindset with which you approach change. There is external pressure to have a plan, but for me it was best not to have one. There were 100 books that I wanted to read and 10 countries that I wanted to go visit. I said to myself, let's just go have fun.*

We advise all sabbatical takers to give themselves a break if they don't get everything done on their list right away. Nancy did just this at the beginning of her break.

> *After two years of working until 10 pm most nights and just generally having no balance between work and life, I left my job as president and CEO of an international non-profit development organization. It had been teetering between life and death when I took the job and was now going to survive. I had given it my all enthusiastically and was ready for someone else to steer it into the future.*

The first thing I did was sleep. In fact, I would sleep long into the morning every day and still be tired. I had various ambitions related to going through boxes from the office and organizing other things around the house, but I didn't have the motivation. I worried that my whole break would be wasted on sleep and doing odds and ends around the house. The only energy I expended was on planning a trip, which gave me something to focus on. I knew the trip would inspire and recharge me. After the first thirty days I was off to Argentina and already feeling better.

CLEAR/ORGANIZE

When leaving the hectic pace of work and before launching into something new, we and other sabbatical takers found the need to clear our heads, clear the clutter in our lives, organize our dwellings, and organize ourselves. The first stage is a time to put things in order. Some decided that they wanted to take care of doctors' appointments, clean out that cluttered room, organize three years of loose photos, paint the kitchen, repair a broken bike, or visit relatives. This is a period of letting go, part of a major transition in which one is leaving an old life behind and preparing to be open to new experiences, change, and renewal.

Many people reported gleefully charging ahead with a list of all the things they wanted to organize, clean up, or do. It didn't faze them that the list covered ten years of neglected chores.

Nancy and others sold their homes and handled all the necessary work associated with moving. Nancy says she has never gotten out of this phase and feels like she is in the movie *Groundhog Day*.

I'm not the best person to tell a clearing-out story. You won't hear: "Here's how I did it, and now I'm done." I'm a pack rat, and it seems like my clearing-out never ends. Boxes from two previous non-profit organization jobs. Old financial files (what to throw away, what to keep?). They all cohabited in my previous house and somehow ended up in this one too when I downsized. I did downsize many things to move into my

current house, mostly furniture and old luggage, and did it pretty effi-
ciently, but it just didn't all get done. I even hired an organizer to help
clear out before the move, but I hired her too late in the process to finish.
She came for a few hours at a time for several days. I didn't rehire her for
the new house—silly me. The moving-in process meant newly organized
drawers and closets, which was great, but many boxes found their way
into the extra room.

Some people use part of this organizing time to prepare for the
next phases, Reconnection and Exploration. As you have read, Cathy
spent the first part of her first break planning, packing, and organizing for an eleven-month trip through Asia, including spending time
reading about each country she planned to visit.

EMPTYING THE EMOTIONAL CLOSET

Many sabbatical takers reported needing time to heal from the
breakup of a romance, a divorce, or another sad or stressful experience. Whether it was having time in their own place for the first time
in a very long time or setting up a new home, people talked about
"getting settled."

Leena, whose main story of change and new love was in Chapters
2 and 4, began her sabbatical after her heartbreak by spending a few
months in her home country of Lebanon. She focused on relaxation,
catching up with old friends, and exploring lost relationships. She did
lots of yoga and read several self-help books about mind, body, and
spirit.

For her third Reboot Break, Regan had just returned to the United
States from Bosnia where she was in diplomatic service. "I came home
totally fried," she said. Regan returned to New York just after the 9/11
attacks. "I needed time to find my home and how I would relate to it.
Besides, I was really tired." So she decided to build a Japanese garden.

It became a mental vacation. I was away from political and environ-
mental stress. It was a project meant to create beauty rather than work

to build a nation. Whereas Bosnia was about the macro, the garden was about the micro. It was one of the ways I was able to refresh myself. The garden brought me home in a very concrete way.

Mary, the woman in Chapter 1 who was the first person to take a sabbatical at her workplace, took four months off in the summer from June until September. Who would have known that this perpetually smiling and cheerful friend was being torn apart inside? As a trader on the floor on Wall Street, Mary had witnessed 9/11 firsthand and had lost many friends. She had been grieving over them for the past eight months, and at the same time bearing the burden of other family issues. On top of that, juggling taking her children to school, working under the pressure of a trading floor, cooking dinner, and being a good wife, mother, and friend just got to her.

Just before she started her break she went to a spa for a long weekend. "I needed to start my detox," she said. Then she and her family rented a home in the Berkshires. Her kids went to summer camp while she explored the area and started to explore her inner self. She started to explore many of the deep issues inside that she had never addressed.

I used to drive around the countryside and just cry a lot. My sabbatical was about opening up all the things that I had inside. I was emotionally drained. I needed to do personal therapy, which I had never done before. I never had the time to do it. I was leading such a busy life that I never stopped to feel. I had a lot of issues to face. **For years I kept stuffing feelings and emotions into my emotional closet. I kept adding and adding things, and then one day the closet door just wouldn't shut anymore.**

The other analogy that Mary used is what she called "plaque." Plaque builds and builds. You can floss, but until you go to the dentist for a deep cleaning, you don't address the issue. She said that for the first couple of days you may feel crazy. It hurts while you're getting rid of all those germs, but then you feel great afterwards.

This might be a good time to step back and acknowledge the things that have been on your mind. It often helps to write them down and make a list of steps you could take to empty your emotional closet. Don't force it. You might want to take small steps and set yourself up for success along the way. And remember to congratulate yourself. If you take steps forward and then backward, you are normal. Just keep at it. Remember that you deserve to be able to open space in your mind for new things. Emotional baggage does not have long-term residential rights.

A DAILY APPROACH

Let's turn to how you might approach a typical day. Time and time again people we interviewed said that one of the challenges was the tendency to over-schedule vs. just relaxing. We recommend starting the day with a reflection period. Greg said, "The first two hours of the day are my thinking and reading time. I still get up at the same hour, but I haven't used an alarm clock since starting my sabbatical."

Some people identified the beginning of their break and the lack of a daily schedule as their low points. Susan, the banker you met earlier, realized how structured her life had become by her workday.

On Monday, the first day of my break, I woke up and felt that I should go to the office. My dad had coincidently started his retirement on the same day. I called him up and asked him if he was struggling with that first day as much as I was. We met for breakfast.

An ultra-organized person, Susan found it hard not to have a schedule, so she made one for herself. Regan felt similarly. "This amorphous state, without the requirement to structure my day, left me shiftless and disoriented. It took me three months to leave unstructured time for myself. Afterward it was an irreversible insight."

A friend of Rita's and former CEO who had taken a Reboot Break recommended reading *The Artist's Way at Work*, a twelve-week self-reflection and writing course.

The book introduced me to the concept of writing 'morning pages,' three of them the first thing in the morning. I have been writing morning pages—some call it journaling—ever since. For someone who likes to charge into the day, stopping and reflecting on what happened the previous day—what was significant, how a certain situation was handled—was important. It also caused me to think ahead about that day's activities, which in turn allowed me to mentally prepare for and relish the activities even more. By the simple act of writing the date at the top of the page of my journal, I suddenly remembered that it was someone's birthday. Had I done my normal charging ahead, I would have missed that wonderful opportunity to call that friend or drop them a note on their special day. Which room or outdoor space I chose to write in was also a treat each day. It allowed me to appreciate my environment so much more, to hear the birds at 6 am, to feel the breeze through the trees, to sit in bed as if it were my throne.

Mornings are always a challenge for Rita because they are her favorite time in the day, and there are so many activities that she wants to do in a given time. Writing, yoga, reading the newspaper, reading a novel, gardening, studying Spanish, and other things could all take up four to five hours. During her time off work, she tried to divide her days so that she had reflection time, time for emails or general paperwork and bills, cooking, and one sports activity a day, whether it was yoga, tennis, golf, swimming, kayaking, skiing, Pilates, or hiking. She even snuck in the occasional nap, as many others reported doing. Cathy said, "Each day my goals were to write my morning pages, exercise, reach out to friends, do something career-related, and enjoy downtime."

Another concept in the book *The Artist's Way at Work* is about taking an "artist date" once a week, usually alone. It could be walking in a beautiful field or looking up at the architecture in a city. The date could be drawing, visiting a museum, or going to a show, a dance performance, or a concert. It is anything that awakens your artistic sense. Even those who are not artists have come to love their "artist dates" and ensure that they have at least one a week.

Mark, who left his high-stress New York job for Brazil and working in non-profits, spent his days reading three newspapers first thing in the morning, one to three hours of physical exercise, cooking, exploring, and lying on a beach. In between, he did volunteer work for various NGOs. He liked keeping a schedule of activities, but he also made sure that he left spaces of free time for himself. "The high point of the day was waking up every morning feeling as good as I did, remembering the day before and what I did, what I said, and to whom I said it."

Another common refrain from the people we interviewed is the enjoyment of things that they hadn't done in years. "I read the paper and watched the news, which I had never done." "I spent more time on the beach than I had in the twenty-five years I lived there and enjoyed it more than before." "I could go to dinner without having to be on call." "I had the joy of not having to be someplace at a certain time."

Everyone's definition of what fun is or what they want to clear or organize in their life is different. There is, however, the common theme of taking time for oneself and rediscovering the joy that exists in doing little things. After an initial adjustment, people basked in their freedom. Several people we interviewed actually used the same phrase to sum up how they felt starting their Reboot Break: "It was terrific!" And it gets even better in the Reconnection and Exploration phases.

▶ EXERCISES

Exercise 5-1: What I'll Accomplish

- List five things that you hope to accomplish during the beginning phase of your Reboot Break. Whether it is cleaning out the closet, making overdue doctors' appointments, or whatever you may have been putting off due to your work schedule, tackling these will allow you time to organize yourself and free you up for the next stage of your time off.

Exercise 5-2: Clearing My Emotional Closet

- List the emotional areas that need to be addressed and cleared out in the first phase of the break so you can be open to new exploration and possibilities for your future.

CHAPTER 6

The Heart of the Reboot Break: Reconnection and Exploration

"Twenty years from now you will be more disappointed by
the things that you didn't do than by the ones you did do.
So throw off the bowlines. Sail away from the safe harbor.
Catch the trade winds in your sails.
Explore. Dream. Discover."

—Mark Twain

You have come through the first phase of the Reboot Break. You've stepped off the work treadmill and cleared away some of your clutter. Order may have been restored in closets or the garage, old emails have been purged, and you've worked on your online photo albums. (Or—for those of us of a certain age—precious photos have been moved from a stack of shoeboxes to family albums.)

Now you are headed into the heart of the Reboot Break: the Reconnection and Exploration phases. This period is what you went on sabbatical to experience, and it is usually the most satisfying part of the process. Go in search of your dreams. During the Reconnection phase, sabbatical takers tend to stay closer to home, as they strengthen relationships and go back to old or forgotten but beloved activities. Reconnection is about getting more comfortable in your reboot skin. And once that happens, it's time for Exploration, which is often a time for new challenges and adventure away from home territory.

Kim's break unfolded in a way that clearly illustrates the two stages. At fifty-nine, she left her executive job at the Portland, Oregon, mass-transit system. She had logged eight years there and nearly thirty in other public roles, and she was ready for a break. When she reached the Reconnection stage of her between-gigs sabbatical, she had already organized the basement and done those photo albums. Then she hosted a family reunion, went skiing with friends, and took on new volunteer roles in public service. She and her husband also decided to downsize and move into the city, so she orchestrated the process of selling the house and the complicated move, while also fitting in regular trips to the gym and taking time for herself. Like many sabbatical takers, she wondered how she ever had time for a full-time job.

Moving to Exploration, Kim and her husband traveled to Africa to go on safari and visit their son in the Peace Corps. It was a decided drain on the family savings, but she convinced her husband that it was a "once in a lifetime" chance. Then they ended up moving again, this time from their cramped temporary apartment to another house. Kim was in such a reboot rhythm at that point that she fit the move in around knee surgery, a trip to the Galapagos with her other son, and a jaunt to Washington DC to represent a non-profit at a political event.

RECONNECTION

During her Reboot Break, Jaye was so excited to have time to herself that she was giddy with all the possibilities before her.

After I had settled into a new sleeping and exercise routine, I started calling and surprising old friends. What a thrill! We planned lunches and some weekend getaways to renew our relationships and catch up on years of our lives. Some were divorced, parents had died, illnesses had transformed us, and now we could finally support each other. I was quickly forgiven for not being there as much as they and I would have liked. I also tried to travel somewhere new each month.

Reconnection is a time of expansion too. What does it mean to expand? According to *Webster's Dictionary*, expanding is unfolding, enlarging, opening, or spreading. When you expand yourself, you feed your mind, your heart, your soul, and your spirit.

Reconnection is a time for serious personal growth. Many rebooters described feeling like they were being revived during this period—being brought back to life, to consciousness, or renewed strength.

Most people find that they want to try something new during this phase, from taking up a new sport to art lessons to volunteering. But they also love doing the fun or satisfying things that were crowded out of their working lives. Maybe it's reading a historical novel or the latest magazines, seeing the Picasso exhibit at the local art museum, or spending a summer afternoon hiking with the kids.

Marvin had a blast during the Reconnection phase. He did home renovation projects he'd put off for years, skied on weekdays, read, and learned French. Having the freedom to do nothing or a lot, depending on their mood that day, is a common pleasure of people we interviewed. **Having the freedom to set your own schedule is a gift of time,** and it is one of the most important parts of the Reboot Break, especially in the Reconnection and Exploration stages.

FEEDING THE BODY

If you've been neglecting yourself physically, the Reconnection phase is a good time to establish new habits and even set goals for your health. That might mean jogging or swing dancing, or just getting into the fresh air each day. It can also be a time to test yourself physically by running a road race or trying rock climbing. Rita started her Reconnection phase by taking a yoga class.

Having spent so much time on airplanes, my back was killing me, and I was very stiff. To feel good mentally, I first needed to feel good physically. I soon added a twice-weekly tennis game to my yoga routine. I hadn't played tennis since I was a child. It was a little embarrassing picking up

*a racquet some thirty-five years later, but I had always loved the sport
and the time was right.*

Jan is the journalist you met in the funding chapter. Over the years,
she had stopped paying attention to her health. She ate too much junk
food, she hardly exercised, and she was lucky if she got six hours of
sleep most nights. On her year-long Reboot Break, Jan's first goal was to
build some form of exercise into her life. She chose swimming because
she could tag along with a friend and use her friend's routine to help
establish her own. Twenty years later, Jan is still a regular swimmer.

Feeding the body can mean finally getting rid of a nagging health
problem like backaches. It can also mean being kind to your body by
having a massage, seeing an acupuncturist, or quitting smoking.

For some people, feeding the body simply means spending more
time in the produce department and less in the junk food aisle. Just by
changing your diet, getting enough sleep, and getting a little exercise,
you'll be happier and more energetic, leaving you in great shape for
everything else you'll be doing during the rest of your time off.

FEEDING THE SOUL

Just as feeding the body prepares your physical self for other adventures, feeding the soul gets your mind and spirit in shape. Food for the
soul comes in three varieties: having choices, enjoying the moment,
and clarifying goals.

Having Choices

Reconnection can be all about choices. You choose how to spend
your time, and you can try new things—or not. Rita says:

*I visited at least ten museums during this period. It wasn't that I was
an ardent art lover. Just the opposite. But given the time and freedom
to choose, I wanted to know what I was missing during all those years
of non-stop work when my friends were visiting art galleries. Learning*

about art became a personal goal. As important as the activity itself was, the ability to choose to do it was more important.

A new-found sense of spontaneity can be one of the best rewards during the Reconnection phase. For most of our everyday lives, what we do and how we do it are in large part determined by our bosses, customers, spouses, children, and other important people in our lives. A Reboot Break can provide the simple freedom to decide what you want to do and when and how you want to do it. It can take some getting used to, but we found, as others did, that it can lead to personal discovery and growth.

Gail took time off from her executive bank job to figure out how to move into not-for-profit work. During her Reconnection phase, she watched *The Today Show* every morning and went to the gym every afternoon. But the rest of her time was open to whim. She often had lunch with friends on the spur of the moment. "I was willing to be very spontaneous, and I was unscheduled most of the time."

Gail spent a lot of time on her own. She wouldn't hesitate to go alone to a movie in the afternoon or a Broadway matinee. She visited all the museums in Manhattan and thought nothing of hopping on the subway just to shop at a specialty food store downtown. Her friends said they had never seen her so happy. So many people we interviewed told us they had no idea before taking a sabbatical how much stress they carried all the time. Sabbatical takers are often told they look ten years younger.

Many people choose to add community service or work with non-profit organizations to their schedules during Reconnection.

Betsy, the forty-five-year-old North Carolina orthopedic surgeon introduced in Chapter 3, always felt she had missed out on a key part of community living. As a successful doctor, she never had the time to do volunteer work on a regular basis between medical school, residency, and her long office and hospital hours. It was important to her to serve the community during her time off. "I wanted to see what it was like to be part of my community without the conflicts of work all the time," she said.

Just before taking time off, she had been elected president of the local medical society for a one-year term. During her Reboot Break, she led the organization in creating Project Access, in which each physician in the county agreed to see a certain number of uninsured patients each year. Also, as you'll read later, during the Exploration phase, Betsy deliberately chose to travel to faraway places where she could participate in deeply meaningful and important volunteer projects.

Enjoying the Moment

Buddhists have been preaching mindfulness, or being in the moment, for thousands of years. It means being fully aware of what is going on inside and outside yourself at any given moment. Mindfulness is all about training yourself to put the brakes on all those thoughts running through your head, so you can enjoy what's going on right now—to stop the past and future from stealing your present.

In his book, *The Power of Now: A Guide to Spiritual Enlightenment,* Eckhart Tolle emphasizes the benefits of being present in your life now and creating greater consciousness. He talks of how to access our own power and inner resources to integrate more fully who we are, so we can create a more authentic future.

Ariane, the *First 30 Days* author you met in Chapter 5, experienced significant internal growth during her sabbatical: **"My sabbatical totally changed me—physically and in terms of my energy,"** she says. "I developed a lightness. The biggest change was inner reliance. I have a deep, intimate relationship with myself now. The sabbatical made me softer, more flexible, more 'in the flow' of life, and less fearful."

In our time-starved environment, we often spend more time planning than doing and don't take the time to just be. Reboot Breaks allow the time and perspective for just being and not doing. It might be sitting on the beach enjoying the sunset or the sound of the waves. It might be listening to the conversations around the dinner table with no interruptions. Or it might be painting a still life and keeping your own thoughts still.

Nancy wrote about a time of being in the moment in April 2007.

*I scheduled a trip to the Bay Area for my daughter Rachel's last col-
lege lacrosse home game and her twenty-second birthday. The best air-
fare meant traveling on a weekday and staying an additional day and
a half before flying back home to Washington DC. Being on sabbatical,
I had time flexibility, so I bought that flight. Once I was in California, I
decided to use the extra hours to wander up the California coast.*

*I write this on a perch overlooking the Pacific Ocean, with waves
crashing below me onto a Stonehenge-like rock formation, then sub-
siding into turquoise and white froth before pounding again. I've come
from a wonderful time with Rachel and her teammates and friends, and
am now deep into my own time.*

*Last night, I drove across the Golden Gate Bridge and continued
north. The spectacular drive at sunset flooded me with unexpected
emotions of release and thankfulness. This morning I've loved climbing
across rocks, walking a flowered field, and now sitting here quietly.
Within seconds, I will put my pen down to just "be" here. Later, I will
drive through the peaceful wine country. What a joy. It is giving me such
a peaceful moment to reflect.*

Clarifying Goals

Who says January 1st is the only day you can make a resolution?
Reconnection can be a time to set goals for your sabbatical, or for your
life. Think of it as an extended New Year's Day. It can be a period of
stretching and testing yourself, physically or mentally.

Along with getting regular exercise, Jan, the journalist we met pre-
viously, decided to use her time away from work to explore the concept of "enough."

Jan had always been driven. She was, in fact, a perfectionist. In her
line of work, she had to be. Every day she dove into details and worked
long hours, digging until she had the full scoop.

Jan had all the skills she needed to be a great reporter. But what
she didn't know, especially after so many years of ambitious work, was

when to stop. She decided the most important goal of her break would be to learn when she had done enough. "I wanted to let go of my need to always push myself to do more," she said.

Jan applied and was accepted for a fellowship for journalists at Columbia University. Though she was away from work, she was immersed in classes and studying. So she set rules for herself: she felt herself wanting to study all night, but she forced herself to close the books and just go to sleep. Pretty soon she saw she could get a good night's rest and still get her work done.

Every day, Jan became more conscious of the choices she was making. Over time, she learned that "enough" was really about priorities. Is getting a little more work done more important than a good night's rest? By making everything a priority, Jan was leaving an important element out of her work: herself. When she was able to pull off the superhighway of her career and look around, Jan could see that a little more work definitely wasn't more important than sleep. Quite the opposite.

When she went back to work, Jan became a national assignment editor at CBS, and then an off-air reporter at ABC. Her workload grew and grew. She was bombarded with more information than ever before.

Every day, though, she used what she had taught herself during her break. Instead of making everything a priority, she switched off her autopilot. She still worked quickly, but now she checked in with herself. After a careful evaluation, she pursued some stories and let other less compelling or interesting ones go. Over time, what had been prioritization grew into that all-important reporter skill: instinct.

Jan went on to become a TV anchor, one of the most demanding jobs in the business. "The 'art of enough' is one that you have to learn and use all of the time," she said. "It's not a matter of getting extra credit. It's all about doing something well, mastering it, and moving on."

EXPLORATION

Nancy tells an Exploration phase story that combines a dream and travel time with her younger daughter:

The phone rang in early June, 2008. "Mom, I've got from June 23 to July 2 if you want to go on a trip. Did you say you wanted to go to Morocco?" It was Rachel. She would graduate in a week, and we'd been talking about having a mother-daughter adventure before she started a new job at a solar power startup.

Within two weeks, we were having our own solar power experience on camelback in the hot Moroccan sand dunes. I had had one last major goal on my sabbatical during the Exploration phase before going back to work, and this was it: the African desert. Now I was looking for inspiration as a Berber guide was leading our camels across the impossibly beautiful desert sands at dusk. Our heads were wrapped in bright cloths against the wind and blowing sand. That night we slept outside under the stars before heading back across the dunes—this time bathed in morning light and total stillness—and on to Marrakech and the rest of our Moroccan adventure.

It was an exotic exploration trip, but it could have been a trip to a national park or Boston or Disneyland. The point is that I was on a Reboot Break and had the flexibility of schedule and mind to plan a spontaneous trip with my daughter.

The Exploration phase deepens the personal enrichment and growth of Reconnection. Choices, reflection time, personal challenges, family, and friends all remain part of the picture. This is a period of pushing yourself by trying or learning more new things and traveling to new places, and it is likely the time when you achieve major goals of your sabbatical.

You may find that you use the Exploration period to explore intensively new places in your own mind and self. Rita says, "I am scared of heights, but in Belize a friend convinced me to go zip-lining, swinging through very high trees on a wire, connected by a harness. It was exhilarating. That day I bought a tee shirt that has become my favorite. It reads: **When was the last time you did something for the first time?**

Exploring the World

Many cultures encourage people to take time off for travel. Australians traditionally take a month off each year, often using that time to travel. Young Israelis who have finished their military duty often take a year off to see the world. In the United States, though, few people get more than two weeks of paid vacation a year, and not many can afford to use all of their vacation time for travel. In May 2009, *Digital Journal* reported that the number of Americans who said that they were going to take a vacation in the next six months was at a thirty-year low, according to an April survey. Expedia also found in their 2009 survey that one-third of employees don't take all of their vacation time.

Given the statistics, it's hardly surprising that so many Americans use their Reboot Breaks to travel. Greg, a former CEO, echoed the sentiment of many when he described the first trip he took in his sabbatical: "A month of walking in the English Cotswolds was the longest consecutive time off I had taken in twenty years. It was the only time I can remember when I didn't have to do something else."

Some people hop in a car or rent an RV to crisscross the landscape of their own country that they've never explored. More often, sabbatical takers choose to go farther afield. Trips are as diverse as one can imagine—walking tours in England, foreign language immersion classes in Germany, cooking classes in Thailand, windsurfing in Australia, skiing in Norway, becoming a registered tour guide in Brazil, teaching English as a second language in Guatemala, and visiting the African desert, to name just a few.

Volunteering

Some people incorporate volunteer work into their travel. Betsy, the orthopedic surgeon you read about earlier, wanted to give back during her Reboot Break, even as she was traveling. Her parents had reinforced this value when she was growing up, and two close friends her age had just died. "I felt my mortality," she said quietly. "I felt I needed to do things that were important to me before I died."

At the top of the list was a month-long medical volunteer project in South Africa for Health Volunteers Overseas. Her orthopedics assignment was in an area with no water or electricity. Betsy was deeply struck by the poverty of the area, juxtaposed with the people's generosity and gratitude and the beauty of the countryside. She loved putting her medical skills to use with these people. "The work of this trip was the reason I went into medicine."

Travel often gives people a new perspective on life, and volunteering can bring that new perspective into sharper focus. As part of their year-long sabbatical, British lawyer Nigel and his wife Sarah worked in Trinidad for two months doing environmental conservation work and coaching village children in soccer. They found that their perspective was broadened by living in a new country where everything about daily life was different from back home.

Nigel felt this even more strongly later in his time off, volunteering in Ecuador. He and his fellow volunteers arrived to create a summer camp program for children in a remote village. The village had just been damaged from excessive rainfall, so the group spent the first three days clearing out a mudslide and creating fields and areas for sports.

The camp was a huge success, and for Nigel it offered an important window into village economic realities, fears, and hopes. A little girl, Isabella, especially caught Nigel's attention. She was usually off by herself and seemed awkward with the other children. When Nigel asked about her, the response was, "Oh, she's that way because her family can only afford to send one child a year to school. Schools are free, but the books and other necessary materials add up to $20 a year. Her brother goes one year and then she goes on the alternate year."

Nigel was profoundly moved. His perspective has shifted forever. Back in his law firm, when someone demands a rush turnaround on something, Nigel frequently thinks of Isabella and the $20 annual school fee. "Yes," he thinks, "it's important to you and I'll do my best, but this is not the most important issue in life." Today, Nigel continues to financially support those needier than he and to find ways during his free time and vacations to volunteer. And the summer sports camp set up by a handful a people during their time off from work continues today.

Sometimes it's hard to explain these experiences and their profound effects to others. Mark and Margaret traveled to the Sudan to volunteer with victims of famine. They set up a medical and feeding clinic and later a project for homeless street kids. Clearly what they experienced firsthand was different from most people's everyday experience back in their hometown.

When they returned home, they thought their friends and family would want to know all about their travels and what life was like in a country so different from their own. Instead they discovered that people gave them little time to describe their extensive experiences and volunteer work.

We and other sabbatical takers who traveled to faraway places had similar experiences. Somehow, there is just a little less enthusiasm for seeing those hundreds of photos or hearing minute details about a story that you still feel in your bones, but that is just too remote for others. In time, Mark and Margaret learned to value their experience for themselves and to accept that others wouldn't be able to understand it in the same way.

Exploring the Mind

Many people devote the Exploration phase to learning. Some take language courses. Some enroll in degree programs. Some do it to change careers. Some want to learn new skills that will bring higher pay.

Those who opted out of work to study for a higher degree or more skills training got a bonus: more pay. Some chose further education as a mid-course-correction. Kevin says that at forty-five he was done with the business world and wanted to teach. And he went off to Texas to get his PhD.

Leslie, at thirty-five, says "I'm done with being a secretary who gives all her friends fabulous home decorating advice. I'm going to get a degree and start my own business."

Several people liked their work and planned to return to their positions but felt unchallenged and needed a change. Learning a new skill or language got them excited again.

Chauncey turned a traditional academic sabbatical into an international networking and learning opportunity. He went from an assistant professor of marketing at a business school to someone on a super-charged Reboot Break having exciting and diverse experiences. At the same time, he was enhancing his academic work and benefiting his university.

He began his time away teaching at Beijing University for the fall semester. It was the start of an enduring academic relationship that would enhance his school's China study tours and international curriculum development. In the spring, he taught at the University of Split in Croatia. While there, he initiated an effort to build a center for the multi-disciplinary study of sustainability on the Croatian island of Vis.

Then he got involved with Starbucks to fulfill another of his reboot objectives, completing and publishing a corporate social responsibility (CSR) case study. He also used this opportunity to publish a manuscript on advertising fair trade coffee.

Chauncey summarizes, "Having new and exciting experiences rejuvenated my teaching. Among the other benefits, I got to build a unique laboratory for students to discover and learn global aspects of sustainable management practices. And it provided me access to hard-to-find research data for meaningful academic publishing."

It is less common for teachers in elementary or secondary schools to take sabbaticals, yet the bold ones do, enhancing their skills and their pay.

Wyatt, a high school physics teacher, used his one-year sabbatical to go to graduate school to enhance and complement his existing knowledge. For him, the free time was as important as the time he spent earning his master's degree in environmental science at Brown

University. During the winter recess, he traveled to Thailand for one month, a trip he would not have been able to take without his educational sabbatical. He also used some of that time to explore a career change. He went back to teaching for a year, and then moved to a job in environmental policy. This kind of exploration is not uncommon among sabbatical takers. It's a great time to test the waters of change.

Wyatt wasn't burned out. He just wanted to take a year to do something that he couldn't have done otherwise and enhance his skills and perspective as a teacher. And, of course, the pay increase for the new master's degree wasn't bad—either as a teacher or in his new career!

Many non-academics in the Reboot Break chorus used their breaks for intellectual exploration. The young banker Susan felt stale and unchallenged at work. At thirty, she was the youngest in her group of fifteen at the bank, and the only woman. It was depressing to her that her co-workers had spent thirty-five years at the same desks. That was not what she wanted, so she set out to enrich her credentials.

Susan applied for and was accepted into a study program at the London School of Economics. She found the course material and discussions very stimulating, but equally stimulating was the travel that she was able to do every weekend, using London as her base. Then she traveled to new places for the rest of her year. Susan returned to her company refreshed and rebooted. She has since been promoted twice and is thrilled that her company relocated her back in London for her next assignment.

Sometimes the education on a Reboot Break is less formal. Gary was a senior public relations and communications coordinator who aspired to be a published author of children's books. During his time off, Gary wrote, took a writing course, attended writers' conferences, and searched for a publisher. He also joined a professional writers' organization to meet other aspiring writers and stay abreast of events and opportunities in his area.

A surprise came in the form of photography and a course-correction. Gary had always had an interest in photography, but during this period it blossomed into a passion. He never expected to uncover another creative outlet, but there he was, taking photos all day long. Today he has created a website and has even sold some of his photos. What was a hobby is becoming a new career expression. "It's hard to describe the lightness, the serenity, joy, and creativity I felt—and still feel," said Gary about his Reboot Break.

EXPLORING THE HURT

Robert Frost once said that "the best way out is always through." Sometimes the most important work of exploration is to acknowledge a painful situation, face up to it, and let it run its course. That's not as much fun as learning French or hiking in the Himalayas, but if you're hurting, sometimes it's the only way to heal.

David, the entrepreneur in Chapter 4, found his once-very-successful business suffering from stiff competition from cheaper labor sources overseas. He spent all of his own money trying to stem the company's losses. Instead, he lost everything. Soon afterward, his partner died. When it was over, he was financially ruined and emotionally drained. David thought about finding another job, but in his heart he knew he needed a break, one that would take him to a world totally different from the one he had left behind. He went to Prague.

I spent my days waking up whenever I wanted to and hanging out with whomever. I just spent the time doing nothing but looking at life through conversations with people I would never have met under normal circumstances: people working for Radio Free Europe, bar owners from Benin and Nigeria who were trying to make it in the West, Czech people caught up in the transfer of the country into the European Union. In Prague, time stopped. Whenever anyone offered me an opportunity to do anything, I said 'yes,' whether it was touring the countryside, going to a beer fest, or visiting a castle. My trip felt like something I should have done when I was younger, but I never took time off after college. Not a day off. My time in Prague felt unnatural after working so hard for so long, but it was completely natural.

David had no definite end to his break. He was very much between gigs. He took comedy classes back in the United States and kept working on a book he had started writing in Prague. He was still recovering from the feeling of failure about losing his business.

It takes as long to come out of something as it takes to go in. People give far too short a time to grieving. Same with my company. I had spent two to three years invested in making it happen, building it up, and watching it crumble. It took two to three years for me to come back. What finally ended this for me was the book. It gave me the external validation of a success, which allowed me to say, "I really am good at something and I can now go to my grave with that." No one can take that away from me. And if I had never gone away, I never would have had that. I would have kept spinning my wheels.

Now David is a freelance corporate consultant on technology-related topics, specifically business continuity and "disaster recovery." He is writing his second book.

Exploring the Self

The Exploration phase can sometimes bring isolation and loneliness. Whether your journey is physical, intellectual, emotional, or all three, being far away from your normal network or experiencing a major life change can be scary and lonely. But it can also be a gift, allowing for profound self-discovery and growth.

David, as we mentioned, moved to Prague. "Leaving the country was important," he said. "I had to get as far away as possible so I wouldn't be able to reach into my old life and fall into old habits. The time zone difference helped, as did the physical isolation of the city." For David, being removed from everything familiar freed him to do the things that he had always wanted to do.

Susan, the banker who took time off to study in London, felt similarly, saying, "My time in London was the only time in my life when I had no connections and was so completely by myself. The first week I thought that I had put myself way too far out there. But once I started to meet people and to create a new social structure, I was fine. I started to travel, too. I had felt totally disconnected, but my new environment allowed me 'think time.'"

Like many of the people we interviewed, Susan is a doer. She's smart, efficient, hardworking, and usually takes on several activities at once. But all this "doing" hadn't allowed a lot of time for reflection and getting to know herself. When Susan was forced to be alone, she was able to discover the things that were truly important to her. Susan returned to the same company after her year off, but she switched from portfolio management to hedge funds because of the insights she gained about herself and her needs.

For some people, self-discovery means spiritual exploration. Many begin keeping a daily journal. Some decide to go to a place or participate in a process that will help them get more in touch with their spiritual side. We know people who took classes in meditation and built that into a daily practice. A few stayed in an ashram to learn the benefit of deeper thought in mediation, and others visited spiritual centers or listened to spiritual leaders. Lorraine, a conflict resolution expert, retreated into silent meditation for a week at a monastery in the beautiful Virginia countryside. Speaking with no one but herself and the universe, immersed in the simplicity of her surroundings, she got back in touch with herself and what is important to her.

EXPLORING RELATIONSHIPS

Jaye was looking for an opportunity during her break to get to know her brother's two children better. They were already eight and twelve years old.

Fortunately my brother provided the perfect opportunity to spend a few weeks with his kids while he and his wife spent time together and had their own reconnection. I jumped at the chance. We had a wonderful time together getting to know each other in a way quick family visits would never allow. It was a gift of time for us all.

If alone time is the yin of exploration, relationships are the yang. A sabbatical is a perfect time to connect with the people you love, whether it's traveling across the globe to meet a long-lost parent or getting reacquainted with your spouse of twenty-five years. The extra time is precious, whether with children, siblings, parents, or friends. It can be planned or spontaneous—a family reunion you host or a pickup softball game.

Michael took his first Reboot Break of three months from corporate work at thirty-five. For three weeks he traveled through northern Europe with his new girlfriend. The trip cemented their relationship, and they ended up getting married a year later. When his girlfriend had to return to work, Michael invited his younger brother to join him. Michael explained that they had never really gotten along well because of their age difference, yet they both found that this time together created a great bonding experience.

Michael's other objective for his time off was to meet his biological father. His mother had remarried when he was very young, and he had never gotten to know his biological father. So he traveled to Germany, where he knew his father still lived. He found his number through relatives and called. "Hi, my name is Michael and I think I'm your son." After a long pause, the response was, "Yes, you are." Michael and his father spent four days getting to know each other and sharing stories of their lives. They have become close friends. Michael now goes to Berlin every two years to visit his father and half-brother, another new friend.

Jerry, an executive recruiter in London, had hoped to use his time away from his job to build a second home and get back to competitive sailing. Then he found out that he and his wife were expecting. Sailing would have required spending twelve weekends away from his wife and newborn baby, so he changed course and spent his sabbatical doing things around the house and immersing himself in parenting.

For some, a Reboot Break brings the bittersweet gift of time with a dying parent or loved one. You have the time to say goodbye meaningfully, doing things you might not otherwise have had time for, such as making a scrapbook of your father's life or listening to your grandmother's favorite music with her.

Rod was let go as part of a corporate restructuring. When his father, who lived in a different town some distance away, became seriously ill, Rod was able to travel there often. When he was home, he found he had more time with his grandchildren.

Friends can be an important part of exploration, too. Regan, the diplomat who returned from Bosnia, devoted her three-month break to traveling **"Reconnecting with my friends energized me in ways I never expected,"** she said. Her friends helped her understand what she wanted from her life and her work. "They reminded me of my passions, my skills, my talents, and my dislikes," she said. "My friends reminded me of who I was."

Being with family and friends can be the most reaffirming part of your Reboot Break. Its importance was mentioned by every person we interviewed. It solidifies the base of who we are and what we care about.

Keeping It Simple—Packing Light

You cleared space and put things in order in the first phase, but this phase goes more deeply into simplifying your life. Clearing away more of life's clutter can open you up to new experiences and tune you in to the things that really matter.

Cathy's first Reboot Break was a time of freeing herself and packing light.

It was 1984 and my mother had died the year before. I had spent many trips back and forth to Missouri to care for her and her affairs. I was exhausted both mentally and physically, and felt I was carrying the weight of the world on my shoulders—in fact my back started hurting, symbolic of that. I also had been working on my doctorate, having finished the comprehensives and coursework, and I was having difficulty with my dissertation advisor, who was always giving me veiled hints that if I slept with him, the process would go smoother, never mind that I was married.

Then there was my marriage and problems there that needed focused attention. Everywhere I turned, responsibility piled on. I dreamed of being free, of leaving problems behind until I could get my head cleared. I dreamed of freedom and packing light, both mentally and figuratively.

When my husband and I decided to take a year-long Reboot Break, using some of the money I inherited from my mother, that's just what I did, taking the time to mourn, reassess my career objectives, and be free. We packed one suitcase each—a Kelty frame suitcase that turned into a backpack—and one small backpack, and took off to travel in Asia for nearly a year. It was one of the most freeing times of my life, and I learned the value of "packing light."

Leena, whom you met before, rented out her apartment in London to finance her break. In addition to the joy and enrichment of traveling, Leena discovered the pleasure of "traveling light," telling us, "I liked not having lots of baggage that could weigh me down and being free of the obligations of my home and belongings. It allowed me to focus more on the people in my life and the direction of my life."

This notion of "packing light" or "traveling light" can refer to emotional baggage, too: letting go of a schedule, going with the flow, or being unburdened. By packing a small "emotional suitcase," Cathy, Leena, and others left room for more important travel essentials, such as confidence, belief in themselves, a sense of humor, happiness, and a complete openness to adventure.

Ariane was thirty years old when she left her corporate job to take a year-long Reboot Break.

The job I was in just wasn't what I wanted. I thought that being in charge of venture capital for a major media company would make me happy. I realized in the first thirty days that it wasn't right for me, but I stayed for two years anyway. I had a nudge from the universe when my company merged with another, and I was told I would have had to move to another state. Around that time, I woke up with a rash from head to toe that lasted for a couple of days. All the tests for allergies came back negative. It was then that I first spoke the words to myself, "I am allergic to my life."

One of the first things I did was to go to Italy, which I thought of as a warm and friendly place. I took only a few things with me, mostly books. I also packed light mentally. I lowered my expectations. Everything in New York is big, important, and serious. I wanted to get away from all that.

Ariane didn't have a plan. Her attitude was that things would show up and that the universe would fill the void. For her, it was a real journey of stepping out of control and away from what was expected of her. Change can be scary and threatening. But when you face change head on—as everyone must do on a Reboot Break—something good comes from that change, even if the reward isn't immediate. In her suitcase, Ariane replaced material treasures with what she calls the five L's: Live, Laugh, Love, Learn, and Lighten up. She went on to found a company and write her book, *The First 30 Days*, about how to navigate change. Both draw on the lessons she learned on her sabbatical.

Time alone, time caring for one's physical and mental health, time with friends and family, spontaneity, being in the moment, reaching out to help others, exploring, learning—these are all the pieces of the natural threads of a sabbatical quilt, the pieces of the sabbatical dream.

All these wonderful experiences are individual and yet universal, and they are only a few examples of the endless possibilities. Renewed and enriched, you are ready for the next phase. In our experience, as you turn to looking for a new job or preparing to return to your workplace, the activities of Reconnection and Exploration will continue as part of your sabbatical rhythm—accompanied by a new sense of self-confidence and direction.

* * *

▶ EXERCISES

Exercise 6-1: Reconnecting to Your Life and Yourself

- Make a list of four or five things you'd like to do during the Reconnection stage of your Reboot Break.
- If one or two items had to come off the list, what would they be?

Exercise 6-2: Exploring

- Make a list of four or five things you'd like to try during the Exploration stage.
- If one or two items had to come off the list, what would they be?

Exercise 6-3: Packing Light for Exploration

- If you plan to travel during the Exploration stage, what is the bare minimum that you need to take with you? List the things that you will absolutely need during your journey.
- What are the things you would like to have on your journey within you? (By within you, we mean qualities such as courage, a sense of adventure, joy, curiosity, enthusiasm, and strength.)
- Is any emotional baggage—a romantic relationship gone bad or self-limiting ideas about your life—holding you back from achieving your sabbatical or its goals? Write it down.
- Review the "emotional baggage" list in a week. What might you be ready and willing to let go of?

CHAPTER 7

Renewed, Recharged, Now What?

"The unexamined life is not worth living."

—*Plato*

The fourth stage of the Reboot Break, what we call "Reentry," marks the start of a new chapter of your life. This is one of the most exciting and satisfying parts of rebooting your life, as you assimilate all that you have experienced during your time off and now make time for reflection. It is a time of new ideas, new possibilities, and new perspectives.

Your adventures have ended and reality has set in. What now? You've expanded your time to include things that bring you satisfaction. You've gotten out and explored, reconnected with old friends, and hopefully allowed plenty of time for rest and introspection. To others, it may seem that you have been on a vacation, especially if you traveled to your dream spot in the Exploration phase, but behind all this wonderful time off, there has been some inward caretaking. Now it's time to bring all those experiences together and determine what's next.

Don't rush yourself. Too often, people try to predict what they will do at the end of their time off before they've even started. When your family asks, don't rush to answer. The answer will come when it's time.

Reentry is usually about coming to terms with the end of a wonderful period in one's life. Take the time to absorb the best parts of your break and figure out how to incorporate those experiences into your post–Reboot Break life. You may be getting a little antsy about your financial situation and what you are going to do next. Or you may be thinking about what it will be like to return to your job or begin a new one. This is a time to start to talk to others about work and to go on job interviews. In this chapter we will explore some ways to think about reentering the work world and give examples of how others handled the transition.

Rita had taken a between-gigs break and was now entering the Reentry stage. An old school acquaintance approached her about a full-time job. Rita didn't think she was interested in the opportunity, but the day before she was going to turn it down, she woke up in the middle of the night with the idea of turning the offer into a two-month consulting engagement. It provided her intellectually stimulating and challenging work while still allowing her the flexibility she had grown to love during her Reboot Break. It also gave her more time to figure out what she really wanted to do.

TRANSITIONS

Reentry is a transition. In fact, the whole reboot process can be understood as a transition between your former work and a new lifestyle. Even if you return to the same company, a transition takes place.

The author William Bridges has written extensively about transition. He made his own course-correction when he left his career as an English professor for the field of transition management. Then he experienced an even more profound transition with the death of his wife. His book, *The Way of Transition*, is based on the deeper learning and understanding he forged during that second transition. Bridges describes a three-stage process, starting with the necessity of ending a chapter of your life and leaving something behind. No matter what the circumstances are—the need for a change, the death of a loved one, the birth of a child—the first step of a transition is "letting go." It involves realizing a phase of life is over and that you are moving away from it and into something else.

Letting go is followed by a "neutral zone," an in-between time of self-examination and discovery. This can be an empty and lonely time, or a very creative time, or both. Bridges describes it as a time of reorientation, personal growth, (self) authentication, and creativity. It is similar to the Reconnection and Exploration phases in this book.

The third stage Bridges describes is "beginning again," with all the attendant uncertainty and exhilaration. For us, it is Reentry.

Ultimately, transition results in renewal. Bridges talks about life's imperative to renew itself and says renewal is possible only by going through the process of transition. "Just what causes the timing of these turnings is beyond our knowing," he writes. "All we know is that periodically, some situation or event deflects us from the path that we thought we were on and, in so doing, ends the life-chapter we were in. In order to continue our journey, we are forced to let go of the way we got that far. Having let go, we find ourselves in the wilderness for a time, and not until we have lived out that time can we come back around to a new beginning."

Part of a successful sabbatical is recognizing, accepting, and celebrating transition and change.

REFLECTION

Time for reflection is so important at this stage because it is where the activities and experiences, the emotions and feelings, and the wants and needs come together to pave the path to post-sabbatical life. If you learn only one thing from your sabbatical, it should be to take time regularly and frequently for reflection. We as individuals all too often move from our head to our feet, from thought to action, without spending time contemplating how we really feel about something.

About half of the people we interviewed returned to their same jobs. And of those, about half were burnt out, frustrated, and fed up with their jobs before taking their Reboot Break. It was only by taking time off and going deep inside that they realized that they actually liked their jobs but just needed more balance. Their Reboot Break gave them renewal and an awareness that there were ways to enjoy life and have balance while still being fully engaged in their work.

Susan, the thirty-year-old banker you've read about in past chapters, never doubted that after her year-long break, she would return to the same company. She liked the company and its values but knew that she would quickly get bored doing her old work. She handled her reentry well and shortly after returning was able to negotiate a rotation into a new department where she could be more innovative. Susan credited her time by herself in London:

I had never been so alone in all my life. But that was good for me and allowed me to figure out what I wanted to do next. Without all of my reflection time I would have never been able to create a plan to return to my same company, but in a new city and in a whole new area that offered a lot more creativity.

EXPLORING NEW OPTIONS

When Barbara was ready to think about work again after losing her job and taking a Reboot Break, she chose to go to an intensive three-day session with a life coach. First, she spent a week answering a questionnaire. The coach raised a lot of intense questions that caused her to think about what was important to her. He also gave her the William Bridges book on transitions.

We talked about the free fall, separation, anger, healing, etc. We talked about what made me click. I did a lot of soul searching. I asked myself,

"What would make me click for the next stage of my life?" I needed to move from making my mark to doing something that made me happy. It had to encompass entrepreneurship and creativity, but I knew that I also needed structure.

Barbara decided to kick off her Reentry phase by contacting people and asking them to write testimonials about her. She explained that she was going through a transition and period of self-exploration and that she would appreciate their points of view on what was special about her.

Barbara sent out about forty emails and thirty people responded. That's an incredible response rate. Barbara found their responses not only very informative but also moving and emotional. By providing friends and previous business colleagues the time and space to give her honest feedback, she was able to hear what made her good at her job, what made her special.

Barbara found her ego again. Now she was armed with the right ammunition and clarity to recreate her bio and start talking to recruiters. She spent time formulating her strategy and assessing various opportunities.

She connected with headhunters and women entrepreneurs. In the process of sending her resumes out to recruiters, one of them said that she would make a great recruiter. Barbara thought to herself, "I am a negotiator and a deal closer, and I am flexible." She decided to take a risk and go into this totally new field. She said that the worst that could happen was that she would choose to leave. Plus, her Reboot Break had armed her with better clarity about her own strengths and where best to use them.

Elizabeth is another person who loved her work and lost it in a company restructuring. When she had been let go from a company several years prior to this time, she was scared of being in her home alone all day. She admitted to feeling a bit panicky each time her husband left in the morning. She therefore went straight to job searching without giving herself the gift of time. She quickly found employment, but not her dream job. This time, rather than jumping right back to work, she turned a crushing event into a gift of time. For the first couple of months, she exercised, traveled, reconnected with college roommates, and enjoyed sailing before breaking out to a new chapter in her life.

After much soul searching, Elizabeth reaffirmed to herself that she really liked training sales forces, and it would therefore be a good idea to connect directly with other people who did similar work. Rather than making individual calls or appointments, she attended a Strategic Account Management Association conference.

When she arrived, the name of her former company was printed on her badge. She had to cross it out and handwrite her name. At the beginning of the meeting, everyone was asked to introduce him/herself. She said "A few months ago, I was the VP of Global Accounts for my company. I am no longer with them, and I now contribute to the unemployment statistics. What you see on my badge is code for saying I am trying to figure out what to do next."

Everyone laughed. Elizabeth said it was very extemporaneous and that she didn't know what was going to come out of her mouth. During the first coffee break and throughout the remainder of the meeting, several people approached her, offering ideas and brainstorming about next jobs. It probably helped that she exhibited a sense of humor and confidence as she handled that difficult introduction. She left the conference with several leads. Today she works with one of the firms that she met there.

Upon returning to work, she looked great and was calmer and more confident. It was only after spending reflection and reconnection time during her break that she realized how many people thought that she now displayed a totally different personality. When she talked or even just thought about work, she had always tensed up. With newfound knowledge, she committed to leaving some of that intensity behind as she entered her next career phase.

Many people worry about how they will explain their Reboot Break to prospective employers, especially in a down economy. Professional recruiters confirm our strong belief that it is not a problem, depending on how you describe your time off. **Remember, this is not "time off" but in fact "time on" to invest in yourself.** Employers might be turned off by negative explanations like "I was totally burnt out and just needed time to be by myself and in nature." However, talking about how you bettered yourself, what you learned, and how you expect your new perspective to lead you to be more creative and innovative will work. One hiring manager said, **"The person who has traveled or tried new things and who is open to different experiences and views is exactly the person we want in our company."**

Some other tips for searching for a new career after your Reboot Break:

1. Polish your resume and bio. There are professional services that can help you with this if needed.
2. Remember to do a financial assessment of your current situation and what you need from your next job to help you negotiate.
3. Put your best foot forward by selecting clothing that portrays the image of a confident, put-together person.
4. Think about how you are going to explain your time off. Get your answers ready for other predictable questions, especially any that might worry you.
5. Prepare questions for the interviewers. Remember, you can now choose a job that fits who you are and the quality of life you want to continue to lead.
6. Send thank you notes after each interview.
7. Google yourself. You may be surprised what is out there about you, and you should know.

NETWORKING

After Rita fell into that first consulting gig, she went on to do two more short consulting engagements for other companies. She liked the flexibility it provided her as well as the mental stimulation, but still wasn't sure if it should be her next full-time career move. During her time off, she met with as many consultants as she could to ask what they liked and disliked about their work. How did she find those people to talk to? Networking the old-fashioned way—picking up the phone. First, she called friends to ask them whom they might know. Then she called professional groups with whom she had been associated in the past and asked which members were consultants who might be willing to speak with her.

Here are some tips for Networking:

- Ask all the people you come in contact with if they can suggest an expert who works in a given field that you want to explore.
- Tap in to your parents, friends, neighbors, fellow churchgoers, people you meet at the gym, etc.
- Send emails to friends asking if they know someone in the field you've selected.
- Make your request hassle-free by drafting a paragraph that they can send on your behalf. A sample is "David, a very good friend of mine, is exploring changing careers and is very interested in knowing more about the consulting world. Since you too made the switch from working for a large corporation to consulting on your own, I was hoping that you might be willing to speak with him about the challenges and rewards of doing so."
- Don't forget to tap in to the power of social media for networking. The one most used for work-related discussions is LinkedIn. Enter your profile and remember to add all the key words to cover your new areas of interest. You can say what you are looking for under "status updates." You can read job opportunities there too. Ask former colleagues and bosses to write a recommendation for you. You can also see who has been reviewing your background and looking at your profile under "who's viewed my profile."
- You don't always need introductions to approach people. You can do research online and even write to people you don't know, asking for a brief conversation. Tools such as Google or LinkedIn may be of help. There is a wealth of knowledge out there.
- Once a connection has been made, ask to schedule a brief phone call or meeting, and do not take too much of their time. We find that people are usually willing to give a helping hand.

- Invite the person out for a meal or a cup of coffee. Let her choose and you pay. A face-to-face meeting is preferable.
- Before the meeting, do online research into his or her background and organization. Come to the meeting prepared with knowledge of the field and questions to ask. Remember, you have asked for the meeting, so take the lead. Sample questions might include: How did you get into your field? What do you like about it? What don't you like about it? What are your biggest challenges? What additional research should I do if this were the next job for me? Are there others to whom I should speak? What have I not asked you that I should have asked?
- Think what you can do for this person in exchange. Is there a book or piece of research that you have that you can send to him? Is there a contact you can set up for him to help him in his endeavors?
- Immediately after the meeting, write or type a note to yourself on what you learned in your meeting. Later, after you have met with several people, it will be helpful to be able to refer back to all the notes and to pull out common themes.
- Remember to send thank you notes.

Utilizing this networking phase of her Reboot Break, Rita determined that consulting was not for her. "It was only after I talked to several people that I better understood the challenges of scaling up a consulting business. And more importantly, I realized that at that stage in my life, I liked to be the implementer of recommendations and that I wanted to stay and see people grow and organizations morph."

To her friends' shock, after swearing that she would never work for a large organization again, Rita went to work for a Fortune 500 global company—the one for which she did the first consulting gig. She would not have done so if it were not for her time off and the very deliberate time she took during the Reentry phase to network and then deeply reflect upon what she valued.

Victor is a consummate networker. Victor had taken a between-gigs break, and it was time to focus on what he really wanted to do. He reflected on who he was, what he was good at, and what gave him the most satisfaction. He thought that he wanted something in the non-profit field. He knew that the best way to do research was to go to the primary sources and get answers firsthand.

I reached out to people I hadn't seen in years. I reached out to some I never knew before. People were really helpful and very willing to talk and to give me their time. From each meeting I got a gem of an idea. Talking to all sorts of people was invaluable. Finding out what others valued in work and what they did was key. I listened hard.

Then, when Victor was close to choosing a job with a not-for-profit group, a friend challenged him by asking, "Is that really what you want to do?"

"I had to admit that I wasn't ready to give up the money one can earn in the corporate world," Victor said. As they talked further, Victor realized that he could have a bigger impact volunteering for a not-for-profit and having money to give to them. Victor would not have come to this realization without reaching out to friends and asking for their advice.

MINI-TRIALS AND INTERNSHIPS

After you have done your research and talked to several people, you may be perfectly clear about your next career move. However, if you still have some open questions, one of the best ways to "try out" a career is to ask one of those people you called if you could shadow someone at their company for a day or a week. If longer, perhaps it could be an unpaid internship.

Amy is the young attorney who was let go from her law firm because of the collapse of the corporate litigation department during the recession. She decided that she wanted to explore something totally different from law. She took a two-month Reboot Break to live in Italy and study the language, as well as the foods. She also explored career opportunities via the Internet. One intriguing idea was doing an internship to segue into a different field. She approached a wine-making company about doing an internship with them. The experience included all aspects of winemaking, from crushing the grapes and blending the tastes to bottling to marketing. The internship was unpaid, but it allowed her to parlay her legal and business skills into a new career field. She was offered a full-time position at the end of the internship and is now happily working as head of compliance and the commercial division in the profession she sought during her time off. Also, she has created her own wine and labeling . . . soon to be commercialized!

ONCE YOU ARE READY TO START BACK

Now that you have decided to reenter the workplace, we recommend that you spend some time thinking through how you are going to react to being back in a work environment. If you are returning to your previous job, call your colleagues to find out the highlights of what has happened while you were out. Start to look at emails and key reports that will bring you up to speed so that you do not feel totally out of it when you return. By the way, don't be surprised if you return after several months off feeling as if very little has changed. That happens frequently. Also, think about what you are going to share about your time off and what you don't want to say. Moderation is the key. You want people to be happy for you and to see your new level of energy and passion, but you don't want to sound like a broken record, describing every detail of your time off and making them jealous.

If you are starting a new job, learn what you can about the culture before starting, and set the tone for what people can and cannot expect from you right from the start. Focus on building new relationships and setting boundaries where you can to enable better balance. It is all too easy to get back into old bad habits, staying late every night, working on weekends, giving up personal time when the work can most likely be managed or staffed better. Don't let people begin to expect that you will always be available no matter what. Setting clear expectations is important to do right from the beginning, and perhaps you can be a good role model for others to do the same.

If you are an entrepreneur running a small company or the boss of a larger organization, think about how you might return to your old title but with a more strategic focus. Your employees or key managers have probably gotten along fine without you. After all, haven't you been preparing them for more responsibility all along? Now is the time to let them handle the day-to-day activities so that you can reflect more on what new strategic directions the business could take.

Whether you are reentering your old place of work or beginning a new career, your sabbatical has made you a new person. Think through the ways your priorities have shifted. Take care to protect the insights you have gained. Take time for your friends. Take time for yourself. Take time for reflection.

Susan is one of those people who has a natural tendency to charge into things. Upon returning to work she felt that she had to deliberately schedule "reflection time" as if it were an appointment in her day. So she asked her secretary to block off time weekly to do so. "It made me a better leader and a more strategic thinker."

During your break, you most likely chose to spend your time only with people you enjoy. We all know the workplace is not like that, and you may be reminded of that as you return. You may have an overly demanding boss, a cranky customer with a deadline, or a colleague who just does not seem supportive of you. The beauty of the workplace is that it brings together a mosaic of different personalities, backgrounds, and thinking styles. In fact, diversity among these elements can encourage a culture in which innovation can flourish.

But sometimes people's work styles go beyond a healthy difference in thinking and processing styles. Cathy Allen, in her research for *The Artist's Way at Work* coined the phrase "a crazy maker" to describe a person in the workplace who is long on problems, short on solutions, and drains his co-workers' creative energy. Rather than getting sucked in, take a deep breath, think of one of those picturesque, peaceful places where you spent time during your Reboot Break, and set some clear boundaries.

SABBATICALS ARE LIFE CHANGING. Make the best use of this last phase of your Reboot Break. Take time to consider how your priorities may have shifted, what you've learned, and how you will use your new knowledge and self-awareness in the next phase of your life.

▶ EXERCISE

Exercise 7-1: Exploring Career Paths

- Make a list of five possible career paths you might take, including staying with your current job or field. Prioritize the top three. How would you explore these?
- Make a plan to learn more through networking. To whom might you reach out? Try to meet with at least two people a week, and afterward write down the key takeaways from each conversation.

Exercise 7-2: Assessing Opportunities

- When assessing a work option, first reflect upon your ideal work and make a list of what is important to you. Then make a list of the pros and cons. Under pros, list all of the things you perceive as the positives about a particular career/work option, and under cons list all the negatives or potential drawbacks.
- What is missing? Often people think they only have one choice. By doing this little exercise you can often approach the opportunity and ask, up front, for a few other things that are important to you.

Exercise 7-3: Returning Mindset

- As you prepare to return to work, write down at least three characteristics of your ideal mindset. For example, "I will take time for reflection, friends and family, self, and patience." This is the time to think about how your priorities may have shifted.

CHAPTER 8

Deflecting Sabbatical Robbers

"Knowledge is learning something every day.
Wisdom is letting go of something every day."

—*Zen Proverb*

Now you've made a plan and know about the phases of a Reboot Break. You have goals, timetables, intentions, and you are in charge of it all. Experienced sabbatical takers know this is where the rubber meets the road. Will you really do all those things—and do them on the schedule you laid out? What will interfere with your plans? For every good intention there are as many "Sabbatical Robbers" and traps to lure your attention away. This chapter will describe some and outline how to overcome them.

WHO AND WHAT ARE SABBATICAL ROBBERS?

The actors in this chapter are you and everyone else in your environment—your family, friends, colleagues, and other professional acquaintances. They all can have a role in slowing your progress toward your goals—usually unintentionally—by making demands on you or causing you to use your time less effectively.

Sabbatical Robbers come in two categories: internal (you) and external (everyone else). Here are a few examples:

ROBBERS THAT YOU CREATE:

- You spread yourself too thin by taking on too many commitments.
- You let day-to-day things (household, etc.) take up the time.
- You can't say no.
- You procrastinate.
- You are having too much fun to do the more serious things you planned.

EXTERNAL ROBBERS:

- **Everyone wants a piece of your time because you aren't working.**
- You are a target for helping out with charitable causes or your children's school.
- Your family expects you to babysit because you have so much time on your hands.
- You are the reliable relative in every emergency or need.
- The house needs work, and you are in charge.
- "What about me? I'd like you to spend more time with me."

Recognize these robbers and deal with them!

It should be clear, though, that **one person's Sabbatical Robber may be another person's sabbatical objective or joy.** For example, Jack loved going to the park every afternoon with his grandson while his daughter went to class. One of Jack's sabbatical goals had been to spend more time with his grandson, which was far more important to him than having that time to himself. If his daughter had pressured him to watch the child, and it really wasn't what he wanted to do with his time, Jack might have viewed it as a Sabbatical Robber rather than a sabbatical joy.

Sometimes, too, there are unintended intrusions—the inevitable unplanned life impositions that simply happen, and you can't prevent them. It may relate to you, such as a time commitment that has to be rescheduled from before or after your Reboot Break to the middle of it. Or it might be something that happens to someone close to you, such as your spouse breaking a leg. These circumstances become not so much robbers as incidents to treat with flexibility and good humor.

When You're the Robber

Many of you have overcome much and accomplished much to reach this point. Most of you are having a positive experience, already benefiting from unfettered time to relax, enjoy nature, clear away clutter, explore and try new things, see friends, be spontaneous. Whatever stage you are in, some of you may be experiencing a gnawing continuation of some of the feelings you encountered when you were contemplating this Reboot Break, and those feelings may be interfering with it.

Guilt often is the biggest culprit, in particular, cultural and family guilt. You may feel guilty not to be working, not to be earning money, not to be volunteering more, or not to be taking on a larger role in your family, since you now have time. This manifests itself in your spending more time than you envisioned on professional activities, volunteering, and family support. Some of the activity is self-initiated; some is in response to requests or expectations.

It is inevitable when you are on a break from work that people will think that you have unending free time and ask for more and more of it. Sometimes they just assume that you have the time and want you to spend it as they expect.

You are more vulnerable to others' requests for your time when you are carrying guilt about what you should be doing or simply feeling that you should be doing more. There is also the danger of inadvertently being flattered into what you really don't want to do.

Here is our prime list of Sabbatical Robbers in this category:

- *You*, who can't say "no" to the people who think you have unending free time and keep asking you, even though their requests pull you off your reboot goals.
- *You*, who feel that since you aren't working and have more time, you should take on expanded volunteer roles, even though these roles conflict with your sabbatical plans.
- *You*, who keep working, even though you are supposed to be between gigs. During Martha's academic "half sabbatical," she cut way back on her teaching time but remained at the university, and the space filled up with so much job-related activity that she says, "The sabbatical was really dreadful."
- *You* and your inability to deal well with lack of structure, and as a result either waste time, procrastinate, or let time drift away.
- *You*, who feel that you shouldn't be paying that nanny or babysitter or caregiver or house cleaner or lawn mower since you are no longer working at a job outside the home.
- *You*, who take on the reliable relative role because you have the time to do it, even if it pulls you off the track you set.
- *You*, who are enjoying the luxuries of downtime so much that you don't get to the meat of your reboot goals.
- *You*, who treats your break like a job, rigidly holding to the schedule and asking, "What did I accomplish today?"

Some people found that they traveled too much, which made it more challenging to find downtime and to get to other sabbatical goals. Nigel, a UK solicitor, and his wife scheduled a whole year of travel, but in retrospect would have cut that down, as it got too tiring and all-consuming. You need downtime. Schedule it. Leave enough time for yourself and what you enjoy.

External Robbers

And beware of those external robbers:

- *Your children and/or spouse or partner* who think you aren't performing up to standard because they haven't adjusted their lenses to the fact that you didn't take time off to add on household chores and family responsibilities.
- *Your grown children or others* who expect you to be available for babysitting, driving kids around, and other such tasks. As Marie's retirement sabbatical approached, a relative noted multiple times how nice it would be that Marie would be able to look after her young nephew Jason when his mother had meetings in town. Laments Marie, "I wish they would ask me if this is something I'd like to do rather than making the plan for my time. I want to make my own plans."
- *Bosses or colleagues* who want you to continue expending effort on your former job, or possibly want you to start early with a few tasks leading up to your new job.
- *Acquaintances* who ask you to apply your professional skills to their non-profit organization pro bono.
- *Your child's school* that wants you to head a committee.
- *Your bowling league,* which wants to put you in charge.
- *Your friends, former colleagues, and former bosses* who can't imagine what you do with all that time. Nancy tells the story of when she saw then–Vice President George H. W. Bush a few months after leaving her job as his National Security Advisor to move to Germany in hopes of having kids with her Army general husband. He asked her, "Nance, what do you *do* all day?" "Well, I study German, go to German-American discussion groups, explore Heidelberg, cook good meals, try to get pregnant . . . " It can be hard to explain what you are doing every day to someone you admire so much, professionally and personally, who has always known you in a work context.

RESPONSES TO YOURSELF

Here's where we tackle how flexible or rigid you want to be regarding your schedule, activities, and goals. It is so easy to get caught up in myriad day-to-day things or to keep saying yes.

Cathy observed ruefully partway through her Reboot Break, "I still haven't done art lessons or painting, although I have my studio space cleaned up." The rest of the Sabbatical Sisters heartily congratulated her for cleaning up the studio and pointed out there was still time for art. Indeed, before the sabbatical ended, she had explored her own artwork fantasies and is still dabbling in art.

It is worth it at the beginning and at times during the sabbatical to consider how one stays on track, but said, "Don't keep poking at it. You don't have to keep asking yourself where you are going."

You can congratulate yourself and think about where you are and what you have accomplished to get to this point, even in the face of daily distractions. Of course, you can make course-corrections too, if you wish. As a Latin proverb pronounces, "It's an ill plan that cannot be changed."

Kim overcame her guilt regarding Sabbatical Robbers by realizing that "if I served in all the causes that ask for some of my time, I couldn't have the psychological space to do what *I* needed. If you get too many things on your plate, it's like being at work."

Other helpful tips:

- Remember the wise Japanese saying that you need to take 15 percent of your energy for yourself in whatever you do. If you run yourself dry, you will not have the reserves necessary to do what you need to do.
- If you've come from a highly scheduled work life, you might need a plan (at least at the outset) for how you'll spend your time. To suddenly have totally unstructured time and more time alone than usual can be "like being in a foreign country, and you don't speak the language," observed Margaret. Schedule only

half the day and leave the other half open, allowing time for the unintended. There are ways to learn to become more "in the moment."

Look How Far You've Come

If you are overly self-critical and restless about what you are accomplishing, you may want to perform this exercise to take stock. Some will never feel the need to do it, and others will need to do it more than once.

- Title a blank paper or a journal page *Look How Far I've Come* and date it.
- Write the date you decided to take a Reboot Break, the reasons why, and your sabbatical goals.
- Make a header called *What I've Done to Get Here* and write the steps you took to make the sabbatical a reality. This includes financial preparation, steps to leave a job, living and lifestyle changes, etc.
- Write the feelings or naysayers you confronted successfully to go on your break. Those two sets of things are *big* accomplishments.
- Now, make a header called *What I've Done on My Sabbatical Thus Far* and write those things down, including everything, even the smaller things. Here are some examples:
  - Simple pleasures like reading the newspaper every day or calling someone special more often
  - Spending more time with your mother or children or friends
  - Cleaning out even one drawer
  - Trying something new like yoga, art, metalwork, or carpentry
  - Getting more exercise
  - Saying no to various demands on your time, or increasing your volunteer work
  - Finding yourself letting go of the work or situation you left behind
  - Traveling

You will be amazed at how long a list you can produce, and most likely your list will have some bigger things on it than the examples given. For example, you may already have decided to sell your house or moved or made other major decisions.

- Now, look at your sabbatical goals again and consider whether you are being true to those goals. If you are lagging or off track or want to change the goals, be gentle with yourself as you consider how you are spending your time and whether you want to change it.
- Write these changes in a section called *Adjustments* or *Potential Adjustments.*
- Set it aside and go back to it in a few days to see if you still feel the same way and want to pursue the changes you have suggested to yourself. Be sure to read the entire document you have created.

RESPONSES TO OTHERS

Here are suggested some responses to external Sabbatical Robbers. These have worked for others and may work for you.

- **Have an elevator speech or cocktail party statement at the ready about your sabbatical.** Develop a great way of describing your time off that makes it more understandable to others and gets you off the hook of being called upon to help out. Take Rita's great line: "You can't imagine all the projects I'm involved in." Or you can say, "I'm on a sabbatical between work gigs (or jobs) and I'm taking time off to explore new things." Mark just likes to say, "I'm an activist." We prefer the response: "I'm taking a Reboot Break!"
- **Make up titles for chunks of time to explain how busy you are.** You can say you've got a conference call, which may be a

call with yourself. We suggest being able to straightforwardly say what you are doing, but for some period of time or for some interlocutors, this approach might help.

- **It can take time to fully separate from the job you are leaving, but you may want to give it a limit and stick to it so you can get on with your break.** Martha says stay away from your former workplace. On the other hand, Margaret, whose previous sabbatical took her and husband Mark to Sudan, left her job at the non-profit Snake River Alliance after fourteen years but joined the board to "keep her finger in" and remain supportive.

- **Don't over-schedule your kids just because you have more time to drive them around.** One sabbatical mother we know only schedules two ongoing activities per child, which leaves more time for her, but it also leaves more time to be closer to the children and have more quality time with them.

- **Learn to say "no."** Have a response ready and practiced for the times you will want to say "no." "I'd love to join your board, but I'm really concentrating during this break on xyz, and I need to stay focused on that."

SABBATICAL ROBBER OR GIFT?

Mary Pat gave voice to a worry, saying, "I live in fear that someone I know will get sick or will need me and will take me away from these lovely days and my peaceful pattern." But, as the next story shows, what may seem like a Sabbatical Robber can turn out to be a gift.

Leena's father fell ill in England with a stroke while she was on sabbatical, and she was greatly relieved to have the flexibility to travel and spend precious time with him and help him contend with the labyrinth of the British medical system. Her siblings were working and couldn't do it. Also during this time, Leena met José as she was preparing to move to a new job in Madrid. She thought of not giving the relationship a chance because it could take her off the track she had already set for the next chapter in her life. Instead she said, "Why not give it a chance?" She turned down the job in Madrid, extended her sabbatical, and is now married to José, the love of her life. For Leena, "Both meeting a new man and tending to my father were gifts."

Kim spent a chunk of her break hosting big family events, but, she says, "I was happy to get all these things scheduled when I wasn't working. I looked forward to hosting the family reunion without having to do it at a fever pitch. Some would call it a Sabbatical Robber, but it wasn't for me."

LESSONS LEARNED

Give yourself permission to say "no." Don't be flattered into accepting roles you don't really want. "Keep your ego out of it," says Marvin. Kim's advice is to look for your gut reaction when the request comes. You may be flattered at first, but does your stomach tighten or your subconscious signal a warning about overload? Have a clear set of goals and stick to them.

For her Reboot Break, Kim left one non-profit board, joined another, and turned down several more. The most difficult conflict was being asked to play a major role in organizing an environmental conference that would have national impact. "I knew they needed skills like mine to get it done," she says. "But I didn't want to do it because it would be 24/7. It is important work, and it would have been wonderful to be part of it, but at a different stage of my life. My time off has taught me that I don't want to go back into all that stress. I'm seeing this from the standpoint of how hard it is to do it, rather than the challenge and glory that I would have loved before."

Make time for yourself and realize that it's okay to take the time. You've earned it. You are doing something important. It's part of a life cycle. In the book *How to Get What You Want and Want What You Have*, author John Gray talks about having to be happy in all aspects of your life to be happy overall. You need a balance, which includes time for yourself, especially on a sabbatical. Absorb this and make it your own.

Keep your goals clearly in mind. You may choose not to stick to those goals, but that should be a mindful decision.

Reframe feelings of cultural and family guilt. One solution is to give family members a role in your sabbatical. Ask them to do something they are good at, such as researching travel on the Internet. Negotiate with your spouse about your time away. Cut a deal on chores. Share your time off with your family: take them with you to museums, on trips, or on other adventures.

Learn to do the rockwork first and fill in with the sandwork. Linda, a therapist, tells her clients to envision a big jar into which you must put a pile of rocks and a pile of sand. If you start with the sand, there won't be room for the rocks. If the rocks go in first, the sand can be filled in around the rocks and there will be space for both. Brandon does his writing in the morning when he is fresh and saves routine tasks for the "least desirable part of the day." He says, **"I save the best parts of the day for myself."**

▶ E X E R C I S E S

Exercise 8-1: Identify Your Potential Robbers

- Name the people or forces who might intrude on your sabbatical plans.
- Think through what their requests might be and whether you want to agree.

Exercise 8-2: Practice Saying "No"

- Write down a gracious "no" response to each request you would refuse.
- Practice saying the responses in front of a mirror.

Exercise 8-3: (Tell Yourself) Look How Far I've Come

- As described in this chapter, write down your sabbatical goals, then *What I've Done to Get Here*, then *What I've Done on My Sabbatical Thus Far*.
- Assess whether you are being true to your goals. If you are lagging or off track, consider whether you want to change the goals or how you spend your time.
- If you do want to change, write down the changes.

CHAPTER 9

"You're Taking a What?"
Life with Someone on Sabbatical

"The person who says it cannot be done
should not interrupt the person doing it."

—Chinese Proverb

Rachel found her mother's Reboot Break a little stressful. Nancy started flying all over the country to attend Rachel's college lacrosse games with other dedicated parents and fans—a treat for both mother and daughter. But Rachel soon found she had to remind her mom constantly that she, not Rachel, was the one on a Reboot Break.

Nancy was excited to spend time with her daughter and suggested a mother/daughter trip every week. Meanwhile, Rachel's academic and athletic schedule left her no time for an adventure in Chicago, a drive up the New England coast, or a trip to visit Great-Aunt Ginny.

"Mom!" Rachel would explain, "I have to go back with the team, and I can't just take a day or two off with you just because you have time to spare."

Rachel did like having her mom at the games and hated to ask her to restrain her enthusiasm, but Nancy's free time sometimes evoked in Rachel a sense of uncomfortable responsibility. Nancy wanted

Rachel's constant attention, and Rachel couldn't always comply. Rachel felt some of her twenty-year-old independence threatened as she tried to balance her time between her mother's newfound freedom and her own life as a college student.

It can be challenging to live with someone on sabbatical. It also can be delightful. From the moment of the announcement of the break until the end, some of life's normal rhythms and patterns are changed, and adjustments are necessary by everyone in the family.

This chapter is for both the sabbatical takers and those closest to them. It contains observations, stories, and advice for all. We urge you to share it with your spouse or partner, children, and others who live with you or are very close to you.

FIRST REACTIONS BY LOVED ONES
TO YOUR ANOUNCEMENT

Reactions when the intention to take a Reboot Break is first announced may be "You're taking a *what*?" accompanied by surprise, jealousy, shock, worry, happiness and support, anger, or all of these. These emotions are normal, and in every case everyone wonders how the sabbatical will go—both for them and their loved ones.

Dale, a New Zealander in her late twenties, planned to leave her office job for four months to travel to India. When she announced her plan at home, her parents were shocked. They could hardly disguise their discomfort and disapproval. Their professionally successful and normally responsible daughter was walking out on a small company that depended on her. She had a future there. What was she doing? "That's not how we raised her," they lamented.

Dale tried to tell them that this time off from work was something she needed and longed for, and that she had cleared it with her boss and figured out with him how her work would get done. The company could manage. She would come back as a better, more committed employee. Her future was intact. Her father was unconvinced and quite upset.

Dale's boyfriend, on the other hand, was very supportive. "Tama, my boyfriend at the time, was really keen on my going," she says, "He thought that I worked too much and that my life was imbalanced. Perhaps he just wanted me to get a life!"

When Mike announced his Reboot Break to his wife Myra, she smiled broadly. She knew what it meant: they would be planning an extended community service trip to Costa Rica. As a biology teacher, she had summers free, but Mike worked in real estate. The only holdup in their plans had been Mike's reluctance to ask for time off. Now he had done it, and they could go.

Constance lost her job and decided to take a meaningful break before looking for another. She and her husband were within ten years of retirement, and she wanted to explore possible ideas. She told her husband the news, somewhat proudly, certain that it was a mature approach. Her eyes shone as she talked about the fun she would have and the trips she would take sleuthing out places.

Her joy met stony silence. He was jealous. He would be toiling while she played and worked on their future. Furthermore, he was hurt that she hadn't consulted more with him.

What reactions do you think you will encounter when you announce your Reboot Break? How will you respond to these emotions?

Your First Responses

Communicate with and include your family. **Early communication with loved ones can help set the Reboot Break on a positive course and determine its success.** One needs allies and supporters, not surprised naysayers or Sabbatical Robbers.

To prevent a rocky start, contemplate out loud taking a Reboot Break, so it's not a complete surprise. When you announce your decision, be as comprehensive and clear as you can about your plans and goals, and how your family or significant other will be included. Be open to ideas and changes you could make that still meet your goals.

Talk about expectations on all sides. You will run up against a brick wall if you make it sound like the agenda is entirely yours. By the same token, you don't want to hear relief from your loved one that you can now take over childcare or another major task. At least you want to be able to talk it out when that is suggested. Whatever the initial reaction, you will want to be ready to talk about your ideas and get advice. You will need to plan well for this discussion. Do some of the planning in Chapters 3 and 4 so you can respond to initial concerns about finances, what you will do, what they will do, what you will do together, and your future after your time off. For example, you may need responses like these:

- *Here's how we can do it financially.*
- *No, I'm not going off by myself for the whole time. There will be lots of family time.*
- *Yes, Mom, I'm being responsible in giving up my job. Lots of people do this and end up in jobs they like much better.*
- *Yes, I know what I'm doing. Even though I've lost my job, I am taking time to figure out how I can move into a more satisfying line of work.*
- *Yes, I'm going to take a sabbatical and I want you to do it too, so we can travel together. Now is the time.*
- *Yes, I'm going to take time off now to take a breather before my last years of work. It's time to lay the groundwork for the move to Florida we've discussed.*

SETTING EXPECTATIONS

Your assumptions about what a Reboot Break is and what it can include may differ from those of your partner, spouse, or family members—particularly when it comes to his or her role.

When Alexandra told her husband that she had been let go from her job in education administration, she was understandably hurt and angry. But when she told him, "I'm leaving in two days for three weeks in St. Lucia in the Caribbean so I can do yoga and relax and figure out what to do next," he was shocked.

After Roger recovered a bit, he started to get into the spirit of things and said, "That sounds great. I'll make the arrangements to go with you. We can get someone to stay with the kids. I may join you a day or so after you get there, but I won't be far behind with my swim fins in hand. We'll have a wonderful time together."

"Not so fast," came the reply. "I'm going alone. I need this time by myself to decompress and get over this blow. You need to stay home with the kids."

Sabbatical takers plan activities to fulfill *their* needs. If there is no early and explicit communication about developing the plans and describing the role of the spouse or partner, the spouse or partner will naturally have his or her own ideas of what it means. Roger thought it meant he was going too.

Sudden job loss can upset normal communications. Alexandra usually consulted with Roger on travel and other issues, and they planned together. But, in this case there was less communication than usual.

Alexandra ended up going to the Caribbean alone, but she extended her stay by a week and Roger joined her for the second part of her trip. They figured out that she could continue to take a break from work rather than start looking for a new job immediately, and he encouraged her to think about starting her own business. She did just that a few months later by establishing a consulting firm, and she has been thriving in the change and new challenge.

When asked to describe the most stressful thing for him about his then-girlfriend's, now wife's, break, Paul replied, "I wanted to be with Cathy to travel and explore new things with her, but I had a business to run. I also had my own routines, being one of the 'regular guys' playing tennis. My routines were disrupted, and I was conflicted. I had my own life to live. We had to work at keeping things in balance."

Cathy relates that Paul had those concerns about his time because he envisioned that Cathy would be totally free from other obligations and wanting to spend every day with him. The dilemma was soon solved when Cathy set forth a very busy schedule for her Reboot Break that had less "Paul time" than he expected. He was taken aback at first, but Cathy's written schedule set the expectations, and it worked out well for both of them. The highlight was a month-long trip to France that turned out to be a mini-sabbatical for Paul.

Sometimes there is an expectation—as described in the Sabbatical Robbers chapter—that the person taking a break will have plenty of time to take over childcare and extra household duties. The break taker often has an entirely different expectation of how his or her time will be used. They both see it as free time to be filled, but their agendas are far apart. The only way to deal with this is to get it out on the table upfront and talk it through.

Then there's the expectation of travel and adventures together. We talked to Carol about her husband, Mark's, academic sabbaticals. As a professor and ordained minister, he is fortunate to have taken two sabbaticals and has another one coming up. Clearly, Mark and Carol had differing expectations. Here's a bit of the interview with Carol:

Question: Tell me about when Mark is on sabbatical. How is it for you?
Answer: Every time he takes a sabbatical, I can't wait for it to be over.
Question: Why?
Answer: He says, "Where's my lunch?" I don't do lunch. I have my own schedule. He is underfoot. Also, he never plans for us to go somewhere special. I think of being on sabbatical as being in a special place. We just stay home.
Question: Does he involve you in planning the time off?
Answer: Never.

Carol's answers were somewhat tongue-in-cheek, but they do provide insight into some of the issues for family members that can be assuaged with planning and discussing expectations.

Responses

It is exceptionally important to discuss expectations on both sides. The sabbatical taker must set forth his or her goals and what that means in terms of practical, everyday activities. He should talk about expectations for himself and family members. It should be a discussion, not an ultimatum. It is good to talk about what you will and won't do. For example, "I will spend more time with the kids, but I will not take over their childcare. Please do not cancel those arrangements." Or, "I expect to clean the attic and would love to have your help and advice on a couple Saturday mornings."

The family members should be clear about their expectations and assumptions as well, and ask as many questions as necessary. The idea is to avoid frustration by having open, specific communication from the beginning. This may sound like drudgery, but it can lay the groundwork for similar conversations as the Reboot Break develops. It will certainly help avoid misunderstanding and disappointment over differing expectations.

VOICES OF FAMILY MEMBERS

In our interviews, we heard stories with a range of scenarios—both highs and lows—that illustrate what those close to someone on a break may be feeling. The next story is a best-case scenario, in which assumptions about the Reboot Break matched and worked out well.

Steve was downsized in March from a technology company in Boise, Idaho. His whole unit's jobs went to Taiwan. The workers were let go in groups, and he was the second to last group, so he and Teresa had known that he would soon be out of a job. In fact, Teresa had been looking forward to having Steve home for awhile. He had been in maintenance before he turned to microchip manufacturing, and he was very handy around the house. She wasn't anxious for him to find another job immediately.

Fortunately, Steve had the same idea. He had so many projects at home and at their small cabin that he couldn't wait to get started. He decided to take a break and not look for work right away. Also, he wanted to think about what kind of work to seek next. Teresa thought that was great.

We asked if Steve was underfoot at home, and Teresa said, "Not at all. I loved having him at home. It was terrific that he could do all the little things and also the big projects we had been talking about for years." Steve was most appreciative of how supportive Teresa was of his not working. She kept telling him that he didn't need to rush back to work, that she was very comfortable with his work break. They had the income from her job and could get along, at least for awhile.

In the summer, he started a new job, but it was a false start. Teresa welcomed him back home full time with open arms. She still had the attitude that his being home was highly valuable to the family, not just for the handyman aspect, but also everything related to family logistics, including having family and young grandchildren nearby. "I always thought he'd make a great house husband," said Teresa, smiling. Steve's view, also expressed with a smile, was, "I liked the role for a time, but not that title."

Steve figured out in the course of his Reboot Break that he wanted to return to maintenance, his original field. In November, he started a new job maintaining the dorms at the university. He counts both the layoff and the Reboot Break as positives in his life. Teresa agrees.

Your Loved Ones' Worries and Fears— Some Common Themes

It is not uncommon for worries and fears to creep in during a Reboot Break, not to ruin it, but just to be there as a tension sometimes, often related to how the expectations are playing out. Worries and fears fall into two categories: family members may worry about their loved ones taking time off from work, and they may worry about themselves. Sometimes they express these feelings openly, sometimes they do not. So it is important to be sensitive to both spoken and unspoken worries. Some common ones follow.

Concerns for the Sabbatical Taker

Boredom. *"What will she DO all day?"* Angus agreed that it was time for Kim to leave her current job, but he wasn't so sure about her not taking another. They could manage without the income, but wouldn't she get frustrated or bored without the daily challenge? The boys were in college, so demands at home had diminished. Then they moved—downsized from a home and yard sized for two boys to a house with half the space and in need of serious remodeling. Now it seemed fortunate that Kim wasn't working. She coordinated the moves and the contractors over fifteen demanding months. Angus continued his job responsibilities and schedule as the founder of a non-profit energy business and foundation.

They agree it couldn't have been done if both had been working full time—at least not while keeping their relationship and their collective sanity intact. "We'll never have a leisurely marriage; we're neither of us wired that way," Angus says. "Kim operates at full throttle, whether it's a paying job, a string of non-profit boards, the house remodels, managing a social calendar during the holidays, or all of it at once. I just relax—well, tense up a little less—and hang on."

Kim told him, "This is a very deliberate decision for me to learn and have time to reflect. I have goals, and I intend to meet them. I'll be plenty busy. Don't worry about me. This is the gift of time I'm giving myself."

Career. *"Will she be okay? Will her career be ruined?"* Dale, the New Zealander who went to India on her break, had had a variety of reactions from her parents and boyfriend, both immediately and as the planning developed. Though she continued to receive pushback from her parents, they understood better after she explained, and even became supportive. On the eve of another Reboot Break to India from her job in Washington DC, Dale tells about the first one:

> *My Dad grumbled and groaned and gave me many long lectures about facing up to my responsibilities and letting people down at work. It was a sermon once a week for the four months I was planning my trip. Aaahhhhhh! Just quietly though, I know he was proud of my loyalty to the friend I was going over to India to spend time with. I guess he was worried that I would damage my career by taking time off at a critical juncture. He was also worried that I would get sick in India. He's a doctor.*

My Mum didn't say too much but was quietly supportive. They gave me some money toward my ticket for my birthday, so they couldn't have been too badly opposed.

Dale did a great job of easing her parents' concerns and staying in touch. She emailed them frequently, kept a blog about her activities, sent postcards from every city. She filled them in on communications from her office so they'd know that all was well there and that her boss looked forward to her return. She reassured her parents that she wasn't being irresponsible. And she never failed to remark on her continuing good health in communications to her doctor dad.

Happiness. *"Will he like it? Will it work out for him?"* Victor's son Benedict warily watched his father plan his time away from work. His father was a workaholic, and Benedict only knew him as such. Sure, they had family time, and he got attention from both of his parents, but his dad was a banker and worked seriously long hours. Benedict worried that his dad wouldn't be happy on his Reboot Break. What would he do with all that time? Would he be frustrated or short tempered? Would he plan major projects to reorganize everything in the house and make him help? Benedict just didn't know what to expect.

Benedict was pleasantly surprised. He had underestimated the power of the gift of time, coupled with both planning and spontaneity. Victor really did stay away from the office and endless hours on the computer and on conference calls. And Benedict was the beneficiary! Victor was very happy, and one of his priorities was to spend time with his son. They had a great time skiing, watching special programs on television, and just being together. Also, Victor acknowledges that Benedict's early concerns reinforced his intention of making the Reboot Break truly a time away from work.

Fulfillment. *"Is he doing what he set out to do and taking advantage of this time?* Another worry is whether the sabbatical taker is doing enough on sabbatical and living up to his or her own dreams.

Kurt had an unexpected but welcome Reboot Break. He had worked for over ten years as a psychiatrist specializing in medications. His division at a prominent university medical school closed, and he found himself with the time he craved to remodel the house he owned with his partner, Perry.

Perry's days off were Monday and Tuesday. That time alone at home was precious to him, but now Kurt was there. It caused a little problem, in that he didn't have his time alone, and also he felt that Kurt was becoming too narrowly focused. Kurt had begun to focus on every detail of the house and the dogs, not—as Perry thought he should—visiting with friends and family, going to the museums he had long wanted to visit, or even planning a great trip.

The moment that Perry absolutely knew that Kurt needed to broaden his horizons was when Kurt said, "I'm so glad you are home. The dogs have been following me around and need so much attention. I need a break." Of course, the dogs were acting the way they always did, but their needs had become magnified by Kurt as he felt more and more responsible for everything that went on in the house. Perry said that even his chores were taken over by Kurt. Yes, it was nice that he didn't have to clean on his days off and that Kurt always had dinner ready when he got home, but things had gotten out of balance.

Another story:

Peter, a university professor, took a sabbatical, and his wife thought he was squandering it. He still went to the office and to various university meetings. She worried that he would wake up a few months after the sabbatical and say with unhappiness and regret, "What did I do with all that time?"

This can be delicate. The family member may be dealing with Sabbatical Robbers, mainly that inner voice saying it's not good to be too carefree when others are still working. Or maybe the sabbatical taker hasn't planned well enough and is procrastinating. It is frustrating for the family member, who wants the sabbatical taker to be happy. (Or of course, there's the possibility of simply wanting the loved one less underfoot.) In such cases, it's time to check in about expectations. Is it going as planned? Should there be changes? Is it time to plan something special together?

Personal Concerns

Change. Life changes when someone is on a Reboot Break. It can impact normal roles and even household tasks, as with Perry and Kurt. It might take the form of a lot of attention all of a sudden, as in the Nancy and Rachel story at the beginning of this chapter. And it can create new demands.

Rachel and her sister Sarah thought it was good that their mother had shed the job that kept her at the office such long hours. They loved seeing her happier and loved the rewards. Both girls benefitted from several lengthy mother-daughter trips and lots of wonderful times in between.

But then there were the matters of Nancy's reboot goals and the roles of her daughters, especially Rachel. Nancy had a few clear goals for her time off, including establishing an exercise regimen and setting up new technological devices. Rachel had not realized that she would be called upon in this regard, but she became, as she tells it, her mother's fitness coach and technology consultant. ("Rachel, how do I email pictures from my phone and computer?" "What are the best exercises for increasing strength in my legs and training for skiing?")

"I had to learn how to manage that, " Rachel says, "All of a sudden I had to complete all these manual labor tasks that accomplished my mom's cleaning goals and provide what were essentially technology manuals and fitness regimens for her. Then I heard about all the successes and newfound joys: 'Look what I can do now!' At some point, getting hundreds of photos emailed to me after I taught her how to do it made her accomplishments start to seem less thrilling."

There was also the matter of the move. Nancy decided her break was a perfect time to sell the suburban family home, downsize, and move to the city. The downsizing process, which found Rachel making numerous trips to eBay sellers and the Salvation Army, and performing many feats of manual labor, like packing and carrying numerous boxes, convinced Rachel that she'll never buy another non-essential item in her life.

Both girls were great sports about it all, but a general rule is to be clear in advance about your goals and expectations. It normally doesn't work well to spring major responsibilities or time demands on the people in your life.

Self-confidence. *"Where do I stand?"* There was a bit of this in Paul's reaction earlier in this chapter. The partner wants to be supportive and keep up with time-off activities, and may be a bit anxious about how to accomplish that. Or there may be issues of inclusiveness. "Is my loved one trying to get away from me or just have a growth experience alone? Will I be forgotten in the rush of new learning, new rhythms, and newfound passions? Can I keep up with my partner's new dimensions and explorations as I continue my job and daily routine?"

The sabbatical taker needs to be inclusive. Plan special occasions. Call frequently when away. Email may not be sufficient for reassurance, as it can feel less personal.

Resentment. Spouses and partners who still must work every day may be envious or angry. They may make more demands of the sabbatical taker to do the household chores, run errands, or take care of the kids. Friends may be envious too that they are not on a Reboot Break.

The sabbatical taker who gets this kind of pushback may need to have another conversation about expectations.

A Word on Guilt

We addressed guilt in the Sabbatical Robbers chapter, but it comes up here too. The emotional reaction of those at home can cause guilt and anguish for the person on a break, even to the extent of impacting the quality of the Reboot Break. Again, reassurance and communication are crucial so that the family reaction will be less likely to be emotional and engender guilt. If it involves children and a spouse, the spouse can play a key role in explaining the situation to the children.

Unanticipated Events

Janie's husband, Scott, was grateful that his wife was on a Reboot Break when he was taken ill, but he was concerned that it would ruin her break. "I was so worried, but Janie was wonderful about it. She postponed a special trip that was to have kicked off her leave, and it became something to look forward to as the scheduled time off wound down. It was so great to know that Janie was there for my initial hospitalization and all my doctors' appointments without her having to arrange to be away from work. It was always so uncomfortable for her when she was working to take time off for family matters. I know she would have done it, but it was just better this way. Though it was a down time for us with my uncertain health, we were close and less stressed than if she had been torn between work and being with me. Janie's focus, lack of stress, and time—just the gift of time—brought us through the crisis of my heart attack in beautiful shape."

Reboot Breaks—just like life—have surprises. You need to be able to make adjustments along the way and sometimes change priorities, while still holding on to your goals as much as possible. The best way to accommodate change is to be in open and honest communication with your loved ones and others who are affected.

ADVICE FOR THE SABBATICAL TAKER

These points summarize what you can do during the Reboot Break to make it a positive experience for your loved ones. Remember that, while your spirit is high, your loved ones are facing the same old pressures at work and home.

- Keep talking, informing, sharing, and asking opinions. Respond to resentments or any other reactions. It's a time to be patient and generous.
- Remember to check in with how your loved ones are feeling. They won't always express themselves openly without being asked.
- Anticipate worries loved ones might have about you, about themselves and their role, or about your relationship.
- Make a regular "date" with your significant other.
- Call and email frequently if you are away.
- Involve them in the learning you are experiencing, and share as much as you can. This can be a great time for family trips that are longer than normal vacations, if that is possible. Everyone grows and creates memories when time allows it.
- Be considerate of their time and responsibilities. They don't have the flexibility you have, and they may not always want to do what you want to do. Let them know if you plan to lean on them for major or minor sabbatical goals.

COPING SKILLS FOR FAMILY MEMBERS

And here are some thoughts from us that could be helpful for your loved ones.

- Say how you are feeling, as positively as possible.
- Don't lose self-confidence. Your loved one is not deserting you, but just going on a journey of self-discovery.
- Discuss demands that you think are reasonable to make upon your sabbatical taker as spouse, fellow parent, or significant other, while respecting the reboot goals.
- Ask to be part of the planning and the plan, but give breathing room.
- Ask to be part of changes along the way.
- Plan your own Reboot Break!

- Be understanding and encouraging.
- Enjoy the time together.
- Enjoy the attention—if your parent overly dotes on you and your activities, try to accept it. If you are ill and are able to be with your loved one more than expected, relish it. If you are able to develop a relationship that otherwise might have faltered or been squashed by the everyday rush, bask in it.

To summarize, the sabbatical experience should be positive for everyone involved. We have given lots of advice here, but the main thing to remember is to communicate, which means listening as well as talking. Remember, the other person has a life too. And you can both enjoy the Reboot Break.

▶ EXERCISES

Exercise 9-1: Important Others

- List family members, friends, colleagues, and others who might be affected by your sabbatical.

Exercise 9-2: Addressing Concerns

- Write about the concerns those people might have and how you would address them.

CHAPTER 10

Living the Lifelong Sabbatical

"Learn as though you will live forever;
live as though you will die tomorrow."

—*Mahatma Gandhi*

We have come to the last chapter, and one we think is most important. **Why would we take time off unless we expected it to change us in some positive way, so that we could truly keep living the lifelong sabbatical,** or at least reap the benefits from it?

In this last chapter, we come back to our own stories—how the four of us are using what we learned during our sabbaticals in our everyday life. We include other examples as well. We also give you ways to take mini-sabbaticals of a week or a month until you can plan your next Reboot Break.

We shared with you earlier some of the statistics about the U.S. workforce, but here are more that are relevant to why we need to incorporate permanent changes into our lives, not just a one-time leave or time off from work. The Conference Board, an independent economic research and membership organization, released an extensive report in January 2010 indicating that job satisfaction is at its lowest level in two decades. The report shows that only 45 percent of those surveyed are happy with their work, down from 61.1 percent in 1987, when the survey was first conducted. Through economic boom and bust, the statistics on satisfaction indicate a consistent downward trend.

These latest statistics on job satisfaction point to the need for us to renew and refresh our perspectives, even if it is in short doses. Most of us cannot just leave our positions or change our bosses, but we can change our attitudes. This chapter will focus on how we can build into our daily lives ways to keep perspective, to be grateful for what we have, and plan for what we need.

Clearly, you are not alone. We all are over-committed, over-worked and over-tired—especially if we are trying to balance a career, a family, and our personal lives. And most of us seem to have lives that are unbalanced. This chapter is about keeping our lives in balance and finding ways to enjoy all aspects of life to the fullest.

TEN THINGS TO TAKE WITH YOU FOR LIVING THE LIFELONG SABBATICAL

John had spent six months on a break after leaving a high-pressure corporate position in New York. When he started his Reboot Break, he was burned out and overweight. He vowed that he would change the way he lived his life, if only during the six-month period he was taking off, and he did that. He started playing tennis again, worked out, lost twenty pounds, started eating healthfully, and took time to get to know his family and friends better, as well as taking time to rethink what he wanted to do next. Before he began his next job hunt, he wrote down several things he wanted to keep in his life after he started back to work. One was to stay in shape and the other was to be home for dinner with his kids at least three nights a week and hold Saturdays as family days, no matter what.

I learned a great deal about myself, as well as my family, during my time off from work, and I wanted to keep that knowledge in my heart. I have changed the way I work and am as a person for the better. It is possible to do if you remember how important the lessons were when you had the time to reflect.

So what can we do to change our lives for the better? Following are ten things we found that can make a difference. We learned them from our own experiences as well as from the stories of others. These may work for you, or there may be ten other things that work better. **The important thing is to spend time thinking about what is important to you, and then schedule it into your life, just as you do business meetings or visits to the doctor.**

1. **Start journaling** every morning to capture your thoughts, dreams, concerns. It will help you observe yourself on that "inner journey" and keep you focused on what's really important to you.
2. **Use the Goals Circle Exercise** at the end of this chapter to identify goals you want to achieve in at least six areas of your life. Do the Goals Circle annually and spend time each year assessing where you are with those goals. Carry the short version of the Goals Circle with you.
3. **Schedule time for yourself into every day, every week, every month.** It can be down time to just listen to music uninterrupted. It can be an "artist date" with yourself to explore a museum or park. It can be time to follow your passion. But put it on your calendar just as you would any meeting or appointment.
4. **Practice saying "no" to things you really don't want to do.** It is a skill to learn. It is often hard to do so because of guilt or obligation or fear of being rude. Say "I'll think about it" or "I'll get back to you" if you can't say no right away. Don't say yes right away, even if you want to do something. Practice giving yourself the time to set your priorities, rather than having others set them for you.

5. **Plan longer weekends and evenings out with friends and family.** Get the chores and errands done at other times so when you can take time off, you use it for yourself and doing things you want. Get your family to help out so you're not doing laundry, grocery shopping, or fixing the gate during those times. Alison told us how she set a timer for twenty minutes and got her daughter and son to help sort and organize a closet each day as a family project. Even if it means working late during the week or on other nights or one weekend a month, organize, consolidate, then delegate the tasks.

6. **Plan longer vacations.** Take at least two weeks together and try to do a month every three to five years—or better yet, every year, if you can. Structure it so you are using your time off like the mini-sabbaticals described in Chapter 3.

7. **Simplify, simplify, simplify.** Your office, your closets, your house, your car, your lifestyle. We live at such a hurried pace. And we have too much stuff! Engage your family in this. You can work on one room at a time. Hold a garage sale, sell stuff on eBay. Put the proceeds in your Reboot Break fund. Give things to charity. Don't buy something if you don't need it. Clear the clutter. It will give you the space you need, physically and mentally, to enhance your life.

8. **Pack "light"—both physically and mentally.** Practice carrying on luggage for trips on planes. Do one thing at a time. Use less and carry less with you. Leave the baggage behind. This goes along with simplifying your life.

9. **Try one new thing and take some small risk each week.** By taking baby steps, we build the courage to do more. It can be trying a new food or restaurant, taking a course, calling an acquaintance for lunch. It can be wearing something different, walking a new route to work, or exploring a new neighborhood. Try a new sport. Just do something that stretches you. Not everything will be great or even good, but that is part of the learning too.

10. **Nourish yourself during stressful times.** Ask for help. Don't be afraid of what's ahead. Think more about creating your support network—family, friends, colleagues, church members. Give to get. Be generous with yourself and reach out to others. They need you and you need them.

STORIES OF LIVING THE LIFELONG SABBATICAL

OUR STORIES

Cathy still writes in her journal every morning to keep her focused and to get her ready for the day. She schedules "artist dates" every week to try something new or go to a new place, whether she is home in Santa Fe or on business travel. She carries a "List Book" with her goals and adds to or deletes from it to be sure she is doing some of those things she has wanted to do. The categories include Career, Health, Relationships, Creative, Friends and Family, Philanthropy, Finances, and House Design and Maintenance. She also carries her Goals Circle with her in her purse.

Cathy spends approximately two days a week on The Santa Fe Group, her strategic consulting company, one day a week on philanthropy and non-profit board work, one day a week on creative pursuits, such as writing, and the rest on fun and time with family and friends. She has empowered her employees to do the day-to-day administration and focuses her efforts on ideas, client generation, and strategic senior-executive-level consulting, which affords her more flexibility.

She is, of course, at a phase in her life where she can enjoy such freedom, but still continually has to make sure her work and non-profit involvement doesn't encroach on her creative and relationships time. Learning to say "no" has to be practiced every day!

I plan to trade my house in Santa Fe each year for a house abroad to learn new cultures, languages, and food. Like my fellow Baby Boomers, I

don't really plan to retire. I just want more control over my time and the
ability to continue to explore and learn, to spend time with my family
and friends, to live life to the fullest.

When Rita returned to work from her third sabbatical, it was to be president of a major division of MeadWestvaco, with over 6,000 employees working for her. The challenge was how to manage the responsibilities of the company and still have time for herself. On her time off, Rita had taken up tennis again, learned yoga, spent more time with her family, and reprioritized what she wanted to do with them.

When she reentered everyday life, she had her assistant schedule a half hour between appointments to give her time to reflect, scheduled tennis on Friday mornings for an hour on a regular basis, and did yoga on planes and when she was on conference calls and no one could see her. She also put her family first, asking her boss if he was willing to put her on early in the board meeting agenda so she could make it to her son's teacher meeting, for example, which is rarely done in the corporate environment. In an effort to bring more fun into her workplace, she used the holidays as a reason to have everyone dress in costume for an employee luncheon and lots of laughs.

Today, Rita has a portfolio career. One-third of her time is spent serving as a director on corporate boards and coaching clients on how to find their first board position. A second third is dedicated to her passion—giving back. She is involved in numerous not-for-profit activities. The one for which she spends most time is as past chair and board member of Pro Mujer, a microfinance organization dedicated to helping women and children in South and Central America. The last third is for having fun, and that part includes new activities, such as learning Spanish and salsa dancing, as well as writing this book.

I am working hard at learning to "be in the moment" and enjoying the
little things in life. I have gone to a lot more shows, plays, museums,
and walks this past year. Most important has been the time I have
had to spend with friends and family. Each day I think of my favorite

question: "When was the last time you did something for the first time?"
Yes, I've had incredible firsts, including trips to Ecuador, Jordan, Spain,
and Cuba, attending a sound healing conference in Santa Fe, and
snowshoeing and kayaking. But that quote has a much more profound
meaning for me. Seeing or doing things for the first time includes how
I look at a building that I may have walked by 100 times or how I look
at the quality of the sky. Every day is an adventure and a new learning
opportunity for me.

It isn't easy to change our lifelong work styles, and outside factors often intervene. Nancy went back to work with the intention of
including important habits from her sabbatical in her new lifestyle.
She vowed to take a lunch break every day to get outside in nature and
do errands, and to leave the office by 6 pm every day so that she could
have a full evening. She also set aside special events on the calendar
with her family and friends to keep sacrosanct and looked forward to
relaxing weekends. But she has struggled with keeping these promises.

One big work project derailed her from what was otherwise a successfully balanced lifestyle. Her workaholic tendencies have returned,
but less strongly than before, and she has kept to her schedule of special events, like her college reunion and trips with family and friends.
Weekends are sometimes relaxing and sometimes taken up with work
or other time-consuming responsibilities—the "keeping up with
everything else" that we all have to do. She's relearning firsthand
the importance of putting personal activities on her calendar, such
as going to museums and concerts, exercising, and dinners out. She
knows she needs a better balance between work, other obligations,
and play, and she is striving to achieve it, starting with rereading this
chapter periodically!

You have heard the old adage "practice what you preach"! Well, I am
trying to do that. But it isn't easy to change habits when external situa-
tions make you revert to old ways. It takes courage, consistency of moti-
vation, and a promise to yourself to keep giving yourself the gift of time.
I do think it is important to have a clear set of priorities, and to know

*how to say "no" to requests for your time. I love doing my Circle Goals
in January, then revisiting them from time to time during the year. I still
keep my daughters, Sarah and Rachel, as my top priorities. I'm doing
volunteer projects in Washington DC, and going to the theatre regularly.
One of my main goals is to continue to get out West several times a year,
where I experience renewal through the beauty and open sky.*

Jaye was very concerned about not losing the calm and peace of
mind she gained from her time off, along with a sense of connected-
ness to her full self. Deciding not to go back to a structured corporate
job enabled her to have more flexibility to build in the things that
were important to her. Jaye increased her involvement with the
Harlem Dowling Westside Center, a foster care and adoption agency
in New York City, and now serves as vice president. She spends more
time with her family, especially her younger nieces and nephews, and
sees them every Wednesday for dinner, to keep up with their busy
lives. Jaye spent time on her Reboot Break thinking about what really
makes her happy, and travel was at the top of the list. She now travels
three to four times a year with friends. She schedules events with
friends on a regular basis. Her work is intense, so she needs to balance
her life with more "fun" things to do.

Jaye is incorporating the work we've done for this book—the
research, learning, forums, community building, websites, and blogs—
into her consulting practice, Breakwater Consulting.

*Seven years ago I took a five-day course on living the life you want. I
was obviously ready in many ways to change my life, but I needed the
time away to really look at my work and life and clarify what I wanted
it to look like going forward. I learned through that process and then the
subsequent year off that it is so critical for me to build in little breaks
on a regular basis. I try to take some time off every month to renew and
refresh myself. If I don't, I feel it and suffer the consequences. This has
been one of the most important lessons so far. Seven years later, I am
continuing to do it. I find that, for me to be the best person, consultant,
and colleague I can be, I must take a step back to learn new things,*

refresh my thinking, and stimulate my creativity. It shows up obviously in the work I do.

MINI-SABBATICAL

We talked about the concept of mini-sabbaticals earlier in the book. While a week, or even a month, doesn't count as a Reboot Break from our point of view, these can serve as shorter refresher breaks to build up to taking more time off. The problem is that most of the week, two weeks, or month you take off can get eaten up by doing pragmatic things or stressful travel or too much activity. In a short time period it is also very hard to detach from work. You still carry your cell phone, PDA, and laptop, and invariably use them. The tips in Chapter 3 should be helpful in this regard.

Following are some ideas of what to do with short periods of time off.

THINGS TO DO IF YOU ONLY HAVE A WEEK

1. **Don't travel anywhere—vacation at home** and take day trips to explore the area around you so you do not have the added stress of travel involved.
2. **Don't do errands or chores—structure the time off to do just what you want to do:** read, take a class, go to a museum, host a dinner party, go on a hike, go to movies, write in your journal, have lunch with friends, but DON'T DO CHORES.
3. **Take an immersion course in a culture, language, or art technique, or go to a spa**—ideally close to home with very little travel.
4. **Take an "inner journey" and devote the week to exploring yourself**—see a therapist, a palm reader, an astrologer; read self-help books, meditate, go on a retreat, write in a journal; do yoga, take long walks.
5. **Plan your next Reboot Break**—read this book again, do the exercises and checklists, explore your employer's policies, talk

to people who've taken time off, plan what you will do when you take a Reboot Break, get your financial planning started.

Keep in mind that giving yourself the gift of time has no boundaries. It can be that quiet moment in a park or a day at the beach or a week devoted to following your dreams. Time is our most precious commodity. Use it wisely.

"It was actually taking a month off to rent a house in Umbria with friends on my birthday that gave me the impetus to do a Reboot Break," said Cathy. She had never taken more than two weeks of vacation at a time since joining the corporate world in 1986. Even then, she always had her BlackBerry with her and called into the office regularly.

The most enlightened experience I had during the month off in Italy was how well my staff did, once empowered. I told them I wouldn't be calling in or checking emails. I prepared them for what issues might come up and I empowered them to make decisions. I said I would not second-guess them or punish them if I didn't agree with their decisions, and I didn't. They were fabulous and professional, and the experience did two things: It changed the way I managed to be even more collaborative, and it made me realize I would still have an effective, functioning business even when I wasn't actively involved for a while. It did wonders for the staff as well.

THINGS TO DO IF YOU ONLY HAVE A MONTH

1. **Rent or trade your house for a house in a different part of the country or world**—anything to get you out of your known environment and the temptation or guilt to do chores or follow your regular routine.
2. **Minimize your contact with work.** Arrange it so you do not have to check emails, call in, or go to meetings. Disconnect. If it is absolutely necessary to connect, make it only one time a week

for one hour. Guess what? They can get along without you for that time period. If that is what you fear, reread Chapter 3!

3. **Don't plan a stressful schedule at home or even traveling.** Make time for yourself. Schedule downtime and do different things. If you have to do chores, concentrate them on one day a week. Use the other time to explore, expand, learn—about yourself and the things you've wanted to try.

4. **Plan your time off, or you will end up frittering it away.** Yes, it is nice to sleep late, watch old movies, and read, but don't make that your primary activity. Set goals for what you want to experience and learn. Take risks to do things you've never done. Structure your time so that you get outside your comfort zone, yet give yourself downtime.

5. **Think of taking a month off every year or at least every three to five years.** Make it part of your life.

THE GOALS CIRCLE EXERCISE

How many of us have talked about or written New Year's resolutions only to forget them about two weeks later? Then we go right back to our habits, whether they relate to our health, finances, relationships, or work, which results in lives that are not balanced and are therefore unfulfilling. The Goals Circle exercise is about changing your life and putting it back into harmony and balance.

In the exercise section of this chapter, we're going to ask you to complete a Goals Circle project that will serve as your guide for integrating all aspects of your life and being sure you create a more balanced approach to life. Cathy created this and wrote about it in her book, *The Artist's Way at Work*, after having used it for several years. Now all the Sabbatical Sisters are creating Goals Circles and sharing them with each other at the beginning of each year. The purpose of the exercise is to balance your life around the most important aspects of it for the coming year. The simple chart is just a circle divided into

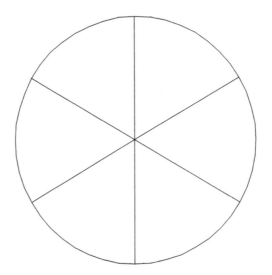

six or eight pie slices of equal size to remind you to give equal time, or at least mental thought, to them.

Label the pie slices on the chart with six to eight aspects of your life. Examples might be: career, philanthropy, spirituality or religion, creativity, friends and family, romantic relationships, health and exercise, education, house renovation, or whatever you have on your horizon for the next year. The categories may be for that year only, such as renovating a house, or ongoing, such as health and exercise. Cathy says:

I usually do this on New Year's Eve or Day, or at least that week. I find a comfortable, quiet place to sit, build a fire, and get my cup of tea and journal or notebook. I first look at what I had said I wanted to do for the past year . . . and I usually have not looked at it for six months. I am always amazed by how much I have accomplished in many areas of my life . . . never 100 percent, but usually 60 to 80 percent, which is great. Somehow, "lose fifteen pounds" keeps reappearing on my lists and never quite makes it off! After reflecting on what I had done and what made me happy, I look to see if I want to include any of the existing categories or goals in the new Circle. I then draw my new Circle and begin to first flesh out the categories, then the goals. Some years I have had as many as twelve pie slices, but I have learned that fewer are better and keep me more focused on what is really important. It doesn't mean that other things are not part of my life or responsibilities, but these six to eight areas should be my real focus for a happy and serene life.

Once you have decided on the aspects or categories, write five goals for each one that are measurable and obtainable in the next year. They may be as specific as "redo my resume" or directional as "travel to a new country," but you should be able to sit down and know at the end of the year whether you obtained them or not.

Here are some example categories and specific goals:

FINANCES:

- Get all financial records entered into a software program like Quicken or Money Management.
- Read three books on financial management.
- Meet with a financial planner.
- Set up a Reboot Break fund and contribute at least $200 to it each month.
- Pay off credit card balances each month.

TIME FOR SELF:

- Schedule an "artist date" each week for an hour.
- Play basketball or tennis once a week.
- Go to a concert or music event twice a month.
- Have a massage once a month.
- Take a golf weekend to learn or improve my game.

It may take you a couple of hours, or even days, to come up with five goals for each category, but it is important to do so to stretch yourself. When you are finished, go back and pick out the one goal from each category that is most important for you to do this coming year and put those on another circle. This circle is one you might carry with you and refer to every once in awhile.

"I recommend putting the larger chart, with five goals each, away for six months, then reviewing it," Cathy says. "Don't try to update or change it . . . just look at it and see where you are against your goals. It is at the end of the year that you want to take the time to reflect." What we have learned from doing this for several years in a row is that most people accomplish more of their goals because they have taken the time to think about them and write them down. The process makes one think about all aspects of life and consider how to keep the parts in better balance. Having five goals in each category makes people think about what it would take to achieve their goals. By spending time planning what we want from life, we are more in control of how we realize those goals. We call it "being present and open" to what comes along. As we mentioned, the Sabbatical Sisters have taken this a step further by sharing our goals with each other at the beginning of the year. The extra step of verbalizing the goals in a supportive environment makes the goals even more attainable. You might try sharing your Goals Circle with a group of friends or family members whom you trust. You can help each other achieve them!

EXERCISES

Exercise 10-1: Ten Things to Do

- Write out ten things you want to include in your life on a regular basis.
- Schedule them into your calendar each week or month.
- Keep the list in your wallet or purse.

Exercise 10-2: Goals Circle Exercise

- Draw your circle with six to eight equal pie slices and categories.
- Put five goals under each category.
- Review it every six months.
- Create a second circle with just the categories and one key goal in each.
- Put that in your wallet or purse and look at it every once in awhile.

Conclusion

We have learned a great deal not only from our own sabbaticals but from talking to so many others who have given themselves the gift of time. Below we share some of the best lessons we've learned about planning for and taking time off. To reboot your life, you need perspective, time for growth, rest, and renewal. You need to be in concert with the natural cycles of life.

Here are some favorite lessons learned by us and those we have interviewed:

- Give yourself permission to take time off—don't be afraid.
- You are not alone; this is emerging as a major trend.
- You will receive many personal and professional benefits.
- There are many benefits to your employers and society as a whole.
- You will want to do this several times.
- You can incorporate what you learn into your everyday life.
- Financial planning is critically important.
- It is important to plan how to handle naysayers, the unexpected, and time robbers.
- Time is precious; don't waste it.
- You will know yourself better after your Reboot Break. The inner journey continues.

Reading this book is just the beginning of the journey. Join us and other sabbatical takers on our blog to share your thoughts and experiences. You can reach us by going to *www.rebootbreak.com* to blog and learn about our upcoming retreats held across the United States. Our email address is on the website as well.

Good luck on your journey!

The Sabbatical Sisters:
Catherine Allen
Nancy Bearg
Rita Foley
Jaye Smith

| APPENDIX |

Planning Checklist

PRE-PLANNING

___ Make the decision to take time off to reboot your life.

___ Begin to keep a journal of your thoughts, ideas, and dreams; write what you want to accomplish.

___ Identify and prioritize your sabbatical dreams and goals.

___ Determine how much time you need on the sabbatical.

___ Tell your spouse, partner, significant other, or friends what you are thinking and include them in the process.

___ Select dates to start and end your sabbatical.

___ Plan when and how to tell your manager, business partner, staff; prepare a script.

___ Have the conversation with everyone who needs to know your plans and discuss the arrangements for the time away.

___ Train staff and make sure there are backups and alternative arrangements for all of your responsibilities.

___ Begin to save and to prepare a budget for your time off.

___ Speak to a financial advisor.

___ Cut unnecessary expenses.

___ Explore alternative ways to generate income (rental properties, selling things on eBay, part-time job or consulting opportunities, etc.).

___ Prepare your house or apartment for rental if leaving on an extended trip.

___ Have all medical exams and doctors' visits before you leave.

___ Sign up for classes that you will want to take.

___ Research places to volunteer, visit, travel.

___ Make sure your passport is up to date if you will travel outside the country.

___ Make flights and other travel arrangements.

You can set up a section in your notebook for plans that you develop. Include a timetable. For example, you might include the category of Reconnecting with Family and Friends. Part of that may be phone calls as well as dinners together. Part of it may involve travel. List these things separately with rough dates.

Create two calendars, starting with a wall calendar to write in your main events, such as travel, classes, and big projects, so you can visualize the main events. The second calendar is the planning calendar, which will be full of planning reminders and event activities. It can be online, on a white board, or whatever works for you. Just develop a system that helps in your process and doesn't end up stressing you out. You need to be able to organize tasks and information for the outcome you seek.

DETAILED PLANNING CHECKLIST

Here are more detailed planning tips that have been taken from scores of sabbatical takers. We recommend, if possible, that you start planning one year in advance of a Reboot Break, but it can be compressed as time dictates. Create your own list that meets your needs. This is just an example.

Planning: One Year Before

▶ *Goal Setting and Research*

- Build a wish list of all the things you would ideally like to do.
- Begin to log and journal your plans, hopes, and dreams. Capture them so that you do not forget. This will be fun to look back over as you get closer and after you have returned.
- Include your spouse/partner in the decision-making process by sharing ideas, hopes, and dreams.
- Involve family and friends in the research of aspects of your sabbatical to share the experience and help to ease their and your anxiety.
- Speak to others who have taken time off or done some of the things you would like to do.
- Map out a plan of what needs to get done and break it into manageable chunks over a year's time.

▶ *Travel and Educational*

- Develop criteria for picking where you want to travel, if you want to travel. This can be to see nearby friends and family, explore a new place in your country, or travel abroad.
- If traveling abroad, research all you can about the country, the culture, and the people.
- Look at websites that offer options for volunteering or working abroad in countries of your choice. (See Resources in this Appendix.)
- Family travel planning is important to start early—*www.suite101 .com* can help you with a wide range of options and information to help you think through the many steps of preparing yourself and your family and selecting places to go.
- Learning about all the possible travel options in itself is a fun project. A good place to start is *www.thetravellerslounge.co.uk.*
- Begin studying a foreign language at home or build that into your plan. There are many options where you can live with a family in country or in reasonable accommodations that the language

schools will provide. To get started, you can check out *www
.languagelearningabroad.com, www.abroadlanguages.com, www.cesa
languages.com, and www.language-learning.net.*

▶ *Work*

- Find out what your company's sabbatical or personal/family
  leave policies are.
- Talk to colleagues who have taken a sabbatical from your
  company.
- Begin to build a plan for transitioning your work while you are
  away.
- Identify who will step into your shoes.
- Document what you are currently working on and what needs to
  be tracked during your absence.
- Plan what you will say to your manager and when.
- Prepare an email (or draft one for your boss) communicating
  your plans to your team, your organization, and your clients.

▶ *Financing*

- Explore options to finance your time off if you are not getting
  paid while away.
- Speak to your financial advisor and begin putting things in place.
- Begin a Reboot Break fund.
- Consider what costs can be cut now.
- See the Funding Your Freedom section in this Appendix.

▶ *Home*

- If traveling for an extended period of time, prepare your house
  for rental or sale. Plan longer-term projects and repairs. Consider
  house-swapping for a while, as another option. (See Resources
  for home-swap websites.)

Eight Months Before

▶ *Travel and Educational*

- Contact and apply to academic programs.
- Apply to special volunteer programs at home or abroad that require an application process and advance deposits to hold your place.
- Look at career sites to get you thinking more about how you will be using your time while away. Some fun career sites include *www.escapefromcubiclenation.com* and *www.gapyearforgrownups.co.uk*.
- Research travel sites to help you book inexpensive housing, such as *www.hostelbookers.com*.
- Teaching English as a Foreign Language (TEFL) is a popular way to see the world and earn as you go. You will need to get certified; *www.online-education.net* can help, as can *www.transitionsabroad.com*.

▶ *Work*

- Cleaning can begin at work. It might be helpful to get rid of unnecessary piles and old project folders to clear the way for others to use your office during your absence. It will also make your office more welcoming when you return, paving the way for new ideas, projects, and energy.

▶ *Financing*

- Contribute to your Reboot Break fund.
- Continue cutting expenses.

▶ *Home*

- Clear clutter and get your house ready for others or identify projects that you may want to do during your sabbatical.
- If renting or swapping your home, there may be things that need to be repaired or adapted for your temporary house guests. It's a

good time to do some of the things that had been waiting to be done anyway.

▶ *Other*

- Practice taking a mini-sabbatical for a week or even just a weekend. Disconnect from your computer and BlackBerry.

Six Months Before

▶ *Travel and Educational*

- Update all passports and necessary travel documents. Most countries will require that your passport be valid for six months past your entry into their countries.
- Check to see if a visa is needed.
- Make extra copies of your passport; carry one with you and ask someone else to hold a copy as a backup.
- If needed, arrange for your children's schooling when traveling abroad or elsewhere in the United States.

▶ *Work*

- Speak to your boss/manager about your desire to take a sabbatical. Present a well-thought-out, positive plan covering what you want to do, why you want to do it, and the advantages and opportunities for the company. Describe your ideas and suggestions about how you will make sure that your work is covered and how others will benefit from the new experiences and responsibilities. Get buy-in from your boss, and after the meeting send an email to both of you that summarizes all that was discussed.
- Begin to implement a training plan for those who will be covering for you while you are away.
- Keep a printed copy of the company's sabbatical policy in case you need to refer to it while you are away.

▶ *Financing*

- Meet with your insurance broker to make sure you have the insurance you need to protect you during your time away.
- Continue adding to your Reboot Break fund.
- Research and prepare to have your bills paid online or through a trusted friend or professional.

▶ *Home*

- If needed, begin your research on storing options for furniture or other personal items you would feel better about storing for safety. While away, you don't want to have to worry about your personal valuables.

Three Months Before

▶ *Travel and Educational*

- Get in touch with people you want to visit if you have not yet done so.
- Begin to think about what you want to pack to take with you on any travels. (Remember to "pack light.")
- Register for any courses or programs that you want to participate in while on your sabbatical.
- Get an international driver's license.
- Buy a railway card for the countries you are visiting.

▶ *Work*

- Train staff who will be taking over during your absence.
- Plan for how your work will be handled and by whom, arrange for and train any temporary help you need while you are away, and make sure your liability insurance will be in effect during your absence.

▶ *Especially For Business Owners, Entrepreneurs,*
and Sole Practitioners

- Figure out who will be running the show and how the work will be handled.
- Arrange for and train any temporary help you need while you are away.
- Make sure your liability insurance is in effect while you are away.

▶ *Financing*

- Make a will or update your existing one, and let people know where you will be and when.
- Set up systems for personal finances and for paying monthly bills.

▶ *Home*

- Work on identifying ways to rent your house or apartment. Start by checking with local real estate agents. Also see listings in the Resources section of this Appendix.
- Prepare your house or apartment for rental by identifying what should be packed and what stays.
- Make doctor and dentist appointments, make sure you are up-to-date on your checkups to avoid any unnecessary health issues.
- Clarify your health coverage for traveling locally and abroad.
- Identify a place to store your car.
- Identify someone to care for pets, and perhaps plants, while you are away.

Two Months Before

▶ *Travel and Educational*

- Arrange for an international calling card. (Once there, get in-country calling cards.)

▶ *Work*

- Build and implement a communication plan for staff and customers/clients.
- Begin to transition things to those who will be working on your behalf and test out the new approach and process.

▶ *Financing*

- Speak to the bank about how to access your money while abroad.
- Automate paying your bills.
- Identify friends, family members, an accountant, or small business services to pay your bills if they cannot be automated, and to handle affairs when you are away. Bills can be sent directly to them.
- Sign and designate a power of attorney.
- Make arrangements for paying taxes if you will be away during tax time.

▶ *Home*

- Pack the house.
- Look into voicemail services so you can retrieve calls while away or arrange for an international cell phone.
- International calling options also might include SKYPE or resources like MagicJack or Vonage. Research and secure a service that is easily accessible and works with your budget.
- Speak to your doctor about getting a six-month supply or more of your medications, and research sources for getting it while away from home, should that become necessary.
- Find out about getting an absentee ballot for voting, should you plan on being away during any election.
- Set up a blog and learn to post pictures and stories there or on sites like *www.snapfish.com or www.flickr.com*.
- Get your camera in working order and get extra memory cards and batteries.

One Month Before

▶ *Travel and Educational*

- Look into and sign up for local classes and activities, such as yoga.
- Get a library card!
- Pack light. You want to be free to move around and not be encumbered by heavy bags and items you don't really need.
- Make sure you have a list of phone numbers and email addresses for all your friends, family, and important contacts, including your lawyer, accountant, plumber, electrician, and anyone you might need to speak to while you are away.
- Check that all of your camera, computer, and telephone equipment is ready to go and charged for action.
- Make sure you have the right adaptors for different electric power if you are traveling.

▶ *Work*

- Introduce the person taking on your role or working in your company to clients and staff to ease the transition.

▶ *Financing*

- Cancel or suspend your newspaper or magazine subscriptions, gym memberships, and any other unnecessary expenses while you are going to be away.
- Suspend your phone service.

▶ *Home*

- Arrange for mail hold or redirection to a friend's or family member's address.
- Arrange for plumbers, electricians, and handymen to be available while you are gone.
- Notify your utility company if services should be suspended for a period of time.
- Do all the grooming you typically like to do (hair, nails, etc.).

Funding Your Freedom

Following are some financial checklists that can help you plan for, and fund, your Reboot Break. Use them to capture where you are today financially and where you want to be while on your break.

▸ **Monthly Fixed Expenses:** *(Create columns for current spending and planned changes)*

Mortgage #1
Mortgage #2
Auto Loan/Lease #1
Auto Loan/Lease #2
Other Auto/Truck Loans
Home Equity Loan
Debt Consolidation Loan/Payment
Student Loan(s)
Rent
Condo or Homeowner Association Fee
Electricity
Oil or Gas Heat
Water
Garbage Collection
Sewer
Phone (land line)
Cell Phones, Pagers, PDA
Cable/Satellite TV/TiVo Boxes
Internet Access
Car Insurance
Health Insurance
Child Support
Alimony
Medical/Dental Payments
Retirement Savings
Emergency Fund Savings
Other

Total Monthly Fixed Expenses:

▸ **Money to Set Aside for Recurring Expenses:** *(Create columns for total amount, monthly savings amount, and planned changes)*

Property Taxes
School Taxes
State and Local Taxes
Quarterly Income Taxes (Local, State and Federal)
Home Insurance
Long-Term Care Insurance
Life Insurance
Car License Renewal
Car Maintenance
Home Repair
Veterinarian
Gifts
Vacation/Travel

Tuition and School Costs
Tithing
Memberships
Charitable Donations
Other

Total Monthly Savings for Periodic Expenses:

▶ **Monthly Variable Expenses:** *(Create columns for current spending and planned changes)*

Credit Card #1
Credit Card #2
Credit Card #3
Credit Card #4
Other Credit Cards
Store Cards
Gas Cards
Other Credit Lines
Groceries
Eating Out
School Lunches
Household Supplies
Gas/Tolls/Parking
Public Transportation
Health Club Membership
Daily Coffee/Snacks
Laundry/Dry Cleaning
Pet Care and Supplies
Baby Items
Childrens' Allowances
Haircuts/Grooming/Manicures, etc
Cosmetics
Clothes

Entertainment (movies, rentals, on-demand, sports events, theatre, concerts, day trips)
CDs
Club Dues
Daycare/Babysitters
Lessons
Field Trips
ATM Fees
Computer/Online Expenses
Donations/Tithes
Lawn Service
Housekeepers
Emergency Savings
Tobacco/Alcohol
Subscriptions
Postage
Other

Total Monthly Variable Expenses:

▶ **Monthly Income Sources:**

Net Income #1 (income less taxes, Social Security, Medicare)
Net Income #2
Net Income #3
Rental Property
Alimony
Child Support
Pensions
Retirement Income
Social Security
Investment Income
Other Income

Total Take-Home Income:

Organizations That Get It

Sabbaticals have long been associated with universities and religious organizations. Over the last decade there have been a rising number of corporations, law firms, service organizations, and not-for-profit organizations that embrace the benefits of sabbaticals or Reboot Breaks.

Below is a list of companies and firms that have implemented some form of a sabbatical program for their employees. The majority of programs were created to offer a fully paid Reboot Break after five, seven, or ten years of service and with an average duration of one to three months. Some programs offer six months to a year. Many other organizations do not have formal programs, but, when approached by employees in good standing, will allow them to customize a personal Reboot Break—while holding their jobs for their return. Hewlett Packard (HP), for example, does not have a formal program, but employees can create their own. At Citibank, one can request up to one year unpaid leave.

In times of economic difficulty, some firms implement temporary programs to help them manage costs while still retaining key talent. Furlough programs offer employees the opportunity to take time off, unpaid or partially paid, but with a guarantee that their jobs will be waiting for them upon their return. Accenture offered such a one-time program. Workers who agreed to an 80 percent pay cut were allowed a six to twelve month sabbatical with benefits. Cisco staffers who accepted a two-thirds pay cut were offered the chance to volunteer at one of twenty-nine pre-selected not-for-profit organizations. Cisco management expected thirty people to take advantage of this program; 300 signed up. In the recent economic downturn, Skadden, Arps, Slate, Meagher & Flom, along with other law firms, paid newly hired lawyers one-third of their starting salaries not to show up for a year. They retained talent while giving their new employees a gift of time.

Some were expected to work pro bono for nonprofit organizations, build experience, and meet potential contacts and future clients.

For more on organizations that offer formal sabbatical programs, visit our website, *www.rebootbreak.com.*

Here is a list of some companies and firms that have implemented some form of a sabbatical program for their employees:

AA Appointments—www.aaappointments.com
AARP—www.aarp.org
Abacus Planning Group—www.abacusplanninggroup.com
Accenture—www.accenture.com
Actel—www.actel.com
Addleshaw Goddard—www.addleshawgoddard.com
Adobe Systems—www.adobe.com
Advanced Micro Devices (AMD)—www.amd.com
Alston & Bird—www.alston.com
American Century Investments —www.americancentury.com
American Express—www.home.americanexpress.com
Ammex—www.ammex.com
Anderson ZurMuehlen—www.azworld.com
Apple—www.apple.com
AppRiver—www.appriver.com
Arco Construction—www.arcoconstruction.com
Arrow Electronics—www.arrow.com
Autodesk—www.autodesk.com
AvalonBAY Communities—www.avalonbay.com
BAIN & Co.—www.bain.com
Barfield, Murphy, Shank & Smith—www.bmss.com
Bingham McCutchen—www.bingham.com
BKD—www.bkd.com
Blast Radius—www.blastradius.com
Boston Consulting Group—www.bcg.com
Brogan & Partners Consulting Group—www.brogan.com
Bureau of National Affairs—www.bna.com
Capital One—www.capitalone.com
CDW—www.cdw.com
Charles Schwab—www.schwab.com
Cirque du Soleil—www.cirquedusoleil.com
Cisco—www.cisco.com

Citibank—www.citibank.com

Citizens Financial Group—www.citizensbank.com

Citrin Cooperman—www.citrincooperman.com

Clark Nuber—www.clarknuber.com

Cleary Gottlieb Steen & Hamilton—www.cgsh.com

Clif Bar & Company—www.clifbar.com

CMS Cameron McKenna—www.cms-cmck.com

Coblentz, Patch, Duffy & Bass—www.coblentzlaw.com

Commonfund—www.commonfund.org

Container Store—www.containerstore.com

Credit Suisse First Boston (CSFB)—www.credit-suisse.com

Daxko—www.daxko.com

Deloitte—www.deloitte.com

Deutsche Bank—www.db.com

Doubleday Broadway Publishing Group—doubleday.knopfdoubleday.com

Drivers Jonas Deloitte—www.djdeloitte.co.uk

Durfee Foundation (finances sabbaticals for non-profit executives)—
    www.durfee.org

eBay—www.ebay.com

Edelman—www.edelman.com

Edward Jones—www.edwardjones.com

Ehrhardt Keefe Steiner & Hoffman—www.eksh.com

Eide Bailly—www.eidebailly.com

Epic Systems—www.epic.com

Farella Braun & Martel—www.fbm.com

FedEx—www.fedex.com

Fleishman-Hillard—www.fleishmanhillard.com

Foley and Mansfield—www.foleymansfield.com

Foster Pepper—www.foster.com

Guardian Media Group—www.gmgplc.co.uk

Genentech—www.gene.com

General Mills—www.generalmills.com

Goldman Sachs—www2.goldmansachs.com

Hallmark—www.hallmark.com

Hammonds—www.hammonds.com

Hewlett Packard—www.hp.com

HLB Tautges Redpath—www.hlbtr.com

Hopping Green and Sams—www.hgslaw.com

Hotel Equities—www.hotelequities.com

Hutchinson Black and Cook—www.hbcboulder.com

Infosys—www.infosys.com
Intel—www.intel.com
John Lewis Partnership—www.johnlewispartnership.co.uk
Joie de Vivre Hospitality—www.jdvhotels.com
Jones Hall—www.joneshall.com
Katten Muchin Rosenman LLP—www.kattenlaw.com
Ketchum—www.ketchum.com
Linchris Hotel Corporation—www.linchris.com
Linear Technology—www.linear.com
Linklaters—www.linklaters.com
Logos Research Systems—www.logos.com
Macdonald and Company—www.macdonaldandcompany.com
McDonald Jacobs—www.mcdonaldjacobs.com
McDonald's—www.mcdonalds.com
McGladrey & Pullen—www.mcgladrey.com
Men's Warehouse—www.menswearhouse.com
Menlo Innovations—www.beta.menloinnovations.com
Microsoft—www.microsoft.com
MITRE—www.mitre.org
Mortenson Construction—www.mortenson.com
Net Atlantic—www.netatlantic.com
New Leaf Community Markets—www.newleaf.com
Newsweek—www.newsweek.com
Nike—www.nike.com
Norton Rose—www.nortonrose.com
NRG—www.nrgenergy.com
Patagonia—www.patagonia.com
Peace Over Violence—www.peaceoverviolence.org
Perkins Coie—www.perkinscoie.com
Plante & Moran—www.plantemoran.com
PricewaterhouseCoopers—www.pwc.com
Procter & Gamble—www.pg.com
Quad/Graphics—www.qg.com
QuikTrip—www.quiktrip.com
Ralston-Purina—www.purina.com
Random House—www.randomhouse.com
Recreational Equipment (REI)—www.rei.com
Reznick Group—www.reznickgroup.com
Robert W. Baird—www.rwbaird.com
Rossetti—www.rossetti.com

RSM McGladrey—www.mcgladrey.com
Russell Investments—www.russell.com
Satyam Technologies—www.satyamtechnologies.net
S.C. Johnson & Son—www.scjohnson.com
Scholastic—www.scholastic.com
Schroder Investment Management—www.schroders.com
Seattle-Northwest Securities—www.snwsc.com
Segal—www.segalco.com
Seventh Generation—www.seventhgeneration.com
Shearman & Sterling—www.shearman.com
Silicon Graphics—www.sgi.com
Skadden, Arps, Slate, Meagher & Flom—www.skadden.com
Standing Partnership—www.standingpr.com
Stayner Bates & Jensen—www.stayner.com
Strategic Actions for a Just Economy (SAJE)—www.saje.net
The Sun—www.thesun.co.uk
Sybase—www.sybase.com
Text 100—www.text100.com
Timberland—www.timberland.com
Unicef UK—www.unicef.org.uk
United States Navy—www.navy.mil
Vauxhall—www.vauxhall.co.uk
Waggener Edstrom—www.waggeneredstrom.com
William Mills Agency— www.williammills.com

Resources

▶ Books:

Bach, David. *Smart Women Finish Rich: 7 Steps to Achieving Financial Security and Funding Your Dreams.* New York, NY: Broadway Books, 1999.

Bishop, Kimberly, Dale Burg and Ginendolyn Penner. *Get Down to Business and You'll get the Job!* Canada: Gemma B. Publishing, 2010.

Bonvoisin, Ariane de. *The First 30 Days: Your Guide to Any Change.* New York, NY: HarperCollins Publishers, 2008.

Bridges, William. *The Way of Transition: Embracing Life's Most Difficult Moments.* Jackson, TN: De Capo Press, 2001.

Cameron, Julia. *The Artist's Way.* New York, NY: Jeremy P. Tarcher/Putnam, 1992.

Cameron, Julia, Mark Bryan, and Catherine Allen. *The Artist's Way at Work.* New York, NY: William Morrow and Company, 1998.

Clements, Dan and Tara Gignac. *Escape 101: Sabbaticals Made Simple.* Canada: Brainranch, 2007.

Dlugozima, Hope, James Scott, and David Sharp. *Six Months Off: How to Plan, Negotiate and Take the Break You Need Without Burning Bridges or Going Broke.* Gordonsville, VA: Henry Holt, 1996.

Ferriss, Timothy. *The 4-Hour Workweek.* New York, NY: Crown Publishers, 2007.

Freedman, Marc. *Encore: Finding Work That Matters in the Second Half of Life.* New York, NY: Public Affairs (Perseus Group), 2007.

Gilbert, Elizabeth. *Eat, Pray, Love: One Woman's Search for Everything Across Italy, India and Indonesia.* New York, NY: Viking Penguin, 2006.

Gray, John. *How to Get What You Want and Want What You Have: A Practical and Spiritual Guide to Personal Success.* Scranton, PA: HarperCollins Publishers, 2000.

Lee, Roberta. *The Superstress Solution.* New York, NY: Random House, 2010.

Levine, Robert. *Power Sabbatical: The Break that Makes a Difference.* Scotland: Findhorn Press, 2007.

Lindbergh, Anne Morrow. *Gift from the Sea.* New York, NY: Knopf Doubleday, 1955.

Savage, Terry. *The Savage Number: How Much Money Do You Need to Retire?* New York, NY: John Wiley & Sons, Inc., 2005.

Sedlar, Jeri, and Rick Miners. *Don't Retire, Rewire: 5 Steps to Fulfilling Work That Fuels Your Passion, Suits Your Personality, or Fills Your Pocket.* New York, NY: Alpha Books, 2003.

Smith, Jaye, and Dina von Zweck. *Venus Unbound: A Guide to Actualizing the Power of Being Female.* New York, NY: Simon & Schuster, 1989.

Stanny, Barbara. *Secrets of Six Figure Women: Surprising Strategies to Up Your Earnings and Change Your Life.* New York, NY: HarperCollins, 2002.

Tolle, Eckhart. *The Power of Now: A Guide to Spiritual Enlightenment.* Canada: Namaste Publishing, Inc., 1997.

Tracy, Brian. *Eat That Frog!: 21 Great Ways to Stop Procrastinating and Get More Done in Less Time.* San Francisco, CA: Berrett-Koehler, 2006.

White Papers:

Allen, Catherine, Leslie Mitchell, and Janey Place. "The New Consumer Value: Living Light." White paper by The Santa Fe Group, 2008. See *www.santa-fe-group.com/wp-content/uploads//2010/07/NewConsumer ValueNove2008.pdf.*

Allen, Catherine, Nancy Bearg, Rita Foley, and Jaye Smith. "Job Loss: Turning Downtime into Your Time." White paper by The Santa Fe Group, 2009. See *www.santa-fe-group.com/wp-content/uploads//2010/07/ SFG-WhitePaper-Sabbatical-Mar2009.pdf.*

▶ Sources of Information on Financial Planning and Budgeting

Magazines and Newsletters:

Consumer Reports Money Advisor
Smart Money
Money Magazine

Websites:

www.bankrate.com
www.betterbudgeting.com

www.billshrink.com
www.consumerreports.org/cro/money/index
www.mint.com
www.money.cnn.com/tools
www.myfico.com
www.nfcc.org
www.savingforcollege.com
www.smartmoney.com
www.terrysavage.com

▶ Sources of Information on Planning for Time Off:

www.encore.org
www.first30days.com
www.gapyearforgrownups.co.uk
www.rebootbreak.com
www.retiredbrains.com
www.thecareerbreaksite.com

▶ Sources of Information on Renting/Trading Homes and Apartments:

www.cyberrentals.com
www.homeaway.com
www.homeexchange.com
www.rentvillas.com
www.sabbaticalhomes.com

▶ Sources of Information on Volunteering:

www.abroaderview.org
www.crossculturalsolutions.org
www.enkosiniecoexperience.com
www.vocationvacations.com
www.volunteervacations.com

| INDEX |

| ACKNOWLEDGMENTS |

WE HAVE GAINED SO MUCH from the help of others in creating this book as well as our Reboot Your Life Retreats. We are grateful for the support, insights, editing, advice, introductions, and research that our friends, colleagues, and relatives have provided us. We are particularly grateful to our interviewees, who shared with us their experiences as well as lessons learned, and the retreat attendees, who have shared their dreams and their fears.

A special thank you to Susanna Space, Julie Kline, Penny Peters, Margot Atwell, Eric Kampmann, Candace Ishmael, Julie Koch-Beinke, Lynn Marfey, Lynn Coppotelli, Sandra Poirier Diaz, Linda Lowenthal, Linda Cashdan, Amy Friedman, Carol Carlisle, Robin Slade, Paul Rooker, Sarah Born, Rachel Dyke, Michael and Nathaniel Buckley, Susan Stautberg, and the wonderful members of the Belizean Grove.

| OUR SABBATICAL STORIES |

Cathy's Story

Cathy has taken two sabbaticals, one for eleven months when she was in her thirties, and the most recent one when she was in her late fifties.

The earlier sabbatical was a travel tour of Asia with my then-husband, giving lectures for the United States Information Agency (USIA) and traveling for pleasure. That sabbatical was motivated by my mother's death, a strained marital relationship, and disenchantment with the academic world, where I was an assistant professor of business administration. I had been taking care of my mom from a distance. I lived in Washington DC, and she was in Missouri. She died in September 1983, and I was exhausted and overwhelmed from taking care of her. My husband and I had married in 1980, separated in 1982, gotten back together in 1983, and were dealing with financial and infertility challenges. I was teaching at American University and working on my doctorate. I was growing increasingly disenchanted with the academic world because of the pettiness of the politics. And then there was the implied threat by my dissertation lead advisor that if I slept with him, I would get my dissertation accepted, and if not, well . . .

My first sabbatical was harder to justify to others than the later one. In 1985 sabbaticals were mostly academic-driven, and the go-go corporate world couldn't conceive of the concept. I was mid-career, as was my husband, and people said we were crazy. ("You'll never get corporate jobs." "You are wasting money." "You will end up divorced.")

As it turned out, the sabbatical was one of escape, relief, and renewed focus on our relationship. We planned to take nine to twelve months off, tour Asia, and come back to new jobs. We traveled in Asia for eleven months, lecturing for the USIA on trade with Asia and the United States, how Congress works, and how to market to the US. Between lectures, we traveled throughout fifteen Asian countries, absorbing the culture, arts, scenery, history, and lifestyles.

For each country, we read fiction, history, economic development, and cultural publications and met with people in the diplomatic, corporate, academic, and arts worlds. We also traveled by every mode, spent time in villages and small towns, visited tourist sites, and ate native food. We challenged ourselves to learn new skills, such as eating with chopsticks the whole time we were in Japan. We tried new foods, learned local languages (at least some basics), and studied cultural protocols.

That first 1985 sabbatical ended in November. I didn't know what would be waiting when we returned. I had sent my resume to a number of contacts before I left on the sabbatical and told them approximately when I would be back. I had a job interview with Dun & Bradstreet waiting for me—a job I took and which propelled us to move to the New York area from Washington DC, and from the academic world to the corporate. From the 1985 sabbatical I learned that taking calculated risks was good, that taking a sabbatical mid-career was not hurtful to my career, that Asia was going to be a substantial economic power in the future, and that I had confidence from the experience that served me well in the corporate world.

The most recent sabbatical was planned as well. I had taken early retirement from my position as founding CEO of a major financial services consortium. I didn't know what would be next, except that I would be managing my consulting firm, The Santa Fe Group, when I returned from my time off.

This time around, it was a natural break. People understood the reasons I wanted time off—personal and professional—and wished me well. There were no naysayers, except my internal voice saying, "Can you really forego the income for a year?"

The planning for both sabbaticals included setting goals of what I wanted to accomplish, how I might finance it, what steps were needed to take care of the house, finances, work, etc. I am a planner by nature, and I found it almost as much fun to plan and dream about what I would do as it was to go on sabbatical.

For the earlier sabbatical, I spend 10 percent of the time planning, packing, and organizing for the trip, 20 percent reading about the country, 20 percent speaking at USIA events, and 50 percent traveling, touring, and enjoying the culture. The 2007 sabbatical was less specific in time. I spent most of the first month and a half sorting and organizing stuff in Santa Fe, working 20 percent of the time on Santa Fe Group/career issues, exercising, reading, and traveling and being with my soon-to-be husband. We spent the month of July in France sightseeing with friends. Each day my goals were to write, exercise, reach out to friends, do something career-related, and enjoy downtime and reflection.

In this recent sabbatical, I was mostly relieved, happy to be free and not in Washington DC, and excited about the journey. I had twinges of worry about finances—mostly because I was building an addition to my house—but I felt confident I'd find a way to earn more when I returned to work.

Had I not taken the time off to reflect, learn, travel, and renew, I would not be where I am today, spiritually, emotionally, and in terms of health. The sabbatical helped me focus my career goals for the next phase of my life.

From the recent sabbatical I learned that planning is important, and having goals and checking in on them makes you prioritize your time. I learned that the hardest thing to do is say "no" and maintain time to just reflect. I am busier than I've ever been, albeit doing things I want to do. I just need to remember to make time for reflection.

NANCY'S STORY

Nancy has taken several sabbaticals during her career in international security and foreign policy. In each case, she resigned from a job to take a break without knowing what the next job would be, and it always turned out well.

After marrying at age thirty-three, when I was in a Pentagon job during the Carter Administration, and then going to the White House to serve as then–Vice President George H. W. Bush's national security advisor, I left Washington to accompany my Army general husband on an overseas assignment. I was thirty-five and wanted to have kids, and it meant leaving the best job in the world after only eighteen months. I missed my career, but I knew I could go back to it. As the two-year Army assignment lengthened into three years in Germany and another three in Japan, so did my sabbatical. It was a time full of discovery and fulfillment: new adventures, travel, language learning, many new international and American friends, public service using my professional skills—and two beautiful baby daughters.

Upon returning to the United States, I took one of those more-than-full-time White House positions at the National Security Council for four years. The girls were then in grade school, and the impetus to take a sabbatical to spend more time with my family was my daughter Sarah's plaintive, "We want you to walk us to and from school like the other mothers do." I did just that, along with volunteering, doing a bit of professional writing, and actually having the time to send out Christmas cards.

Then I mentioned to a friend that I was ready to take on a part-time job, and the non-profit world beckoned with a job that quickly became full-time, as they always seem to. Seven years later, I was still directing the program I founded on International Peace, Security and Prosperity at the Aspen Institute but badly needed a break as a result of the pressures of a divorce, coupled with trying to make it to all the kids' sports games plus everything else. There wasn't enough time and energy (physical and emotional) for work, kids, and a divorce, so I took another sabbatical.

In retrospect, the break from work was too short to get enough recharge and renewal because, after only a few months, I took on a new challenge as president and CEO of a struggling international development non-profit organization. After two years, the organization was on an even keel and I had promises to keep to my family, specifically overseas trips with my daughters, who were now in college, and I wanted to spend time with my mother and with a childhood friend who was struggling with breast cancer. And I wanted to return to the policy world in conflict prevention after taking some time off for myself. So I began another career break at age fifty-seven.

This break was truly one of giving myself the gift of time. There were so many possibilities for family time, friends, travel, some consulting work, non-profit boards, and teaching a university course. I dove into the smorgasbord, though I was living mostly on savings. A major highlight was being with my daughter Sarah in the Balkans where she was studying. Amid it all, the biggest project was moving the family from the suburbs to urban Washington DC, which I believe couldn't have been done if I were working. The time flexibility was fabulous, and it even led to writing this book to share sabbaticals with others.

RITA'S STORY

Rita has taken four sabbaticals over her career. Here is one of her stories.

Four days on the West Coast, three on the East, that is, when I wasn't in Europe or Asia. That is how I had spent the better part of the one and a half years before my second sabbatical. I lived on planes. It was exhilarating, and it was exhausting.

I had been working for a computer company for seventeen years when an opportunity came along to take a software company public. The problem was that I was living in Boston, had a home in Brooklyn, and the job was in California. My husband, children, and I determined that it was a too good a job to pass up. They moved back to Brooklyn and I flew home on as many weekends as I could, except for the summer when one son went to camp and the other came out with a friend to live and work with me in California.

I asked myself, could I handle that type of crazy schedule? Yes, for a while. My life was so segmented between work and family that I threw myself into both. In California my work days started at 7 am after a walk on the beach. They usually ended around 11 pm after a working dinner. I read and did my strategic thinking on planes. Back in Brooklyn, it was cooking and doing family activities.

It was an exciting time to see a young software company grow, to work with a very energized workforce, to be able to conduct business globally, and to be admired by your customers. Yet my life felt schizophrenic. I had a reputation for enormous work capacity and being able to multitask. But inside, my two worlds were tearing me apart. As time went on, I discovered that the founders were having trouble with growing pains and they were learning what it took to be a public company. Our management and strategic views collided. We agreed to part ways.

That was the beginning of October. I knew that once word leaked out that I had left, the phone would start ringing. And it did. But I had determined ahead of time that I needed at least three months to refresh and to reconnect with my life in New York. I politely told headhunters that I was taking a break and would be glad to speak with them after January 1st.

So what did I do? Nothing and everything. My goal was to enjoy the simple things in life, all those little things that my hectic schedule never allowed. First on my list was reading the *New York Times* from cover to cover in the relaxing environment of Starbucks. After that, I either played tennis or went to a yoga class. I did lots of walking, cooking, visiting museums, and reconnecting with friends and family.

In January, the calls began and I did meet with several people. I thought before my sabbatical that my next position would most likely be as a CEO of a technology company or an Internet start-up. But I had lots of reflection time during my time off, and I found that inside I was rebelling from the insidiousness of the Internet and software boom. Make your millions, sell, and get out was not a work model that I had grown up with. It offended my sense of responsibility and business ethics.

I fell into consulting when an old school acquaintance approached me for help with a specific business need. I turned our discussion into a two-month consulting engagement, which gave me more time to reflect and network. I enjoyed consulting and went on to work with other companies. But I soon realized that if I wanted to keep doing what I was doing I would have to scale up my practice and hire help. I met with as many consultants as I could to ask what they liked and disliked about their work.

These discussions helped me realize that consulting was not for me. I like to be the implementer of recommendations. I enjoy seeing people grow and organizations morph. To my friends' shock, after swearing that I would never work for a large organization again, I went to work for a Fortune 500 global company—the one for which I had done the first consulting gig. I would not have done so, were it not for my sabbatical and the very deliberate time that I took to reflect upon what I valued.

Jaye's Story

After seven years as an independent consultant, Jaye was unfulfilled and unchallenged. She was in a rut, and she didn't know how to get out.

My sister was gravely ill and terminal. I knew I needed to find something that was fulfilling but would also enable me to support her three children. After much deliberation, self-analysis, and networking with colleagues who knew me well, I created a new vision of a consulting firm focused on corporate consulting, called Partners in Human Resources International. I quickly found collaborators in that vision. As we built the business plan, we began writing our own ideal job descriptions. Because of the diversity of our skills, we were able to design the company structure around each of our strengths, interests, and goals. I was head of quality control in the delivery of services, consultant selection, and project management, and also in charge of new business.

The company grew quickly. By year five, we had reached $7 million in revenue. One of my two partners decided to retire. That's when things started to change for me. I was thrust into the role of president of the firm, a role more focused on operations, which was not my passion, but where I had capability. As a good partner, I took on the role enthusiastically. I was determined to succeed. We continued to grow.

After four more years, the needs of the company had changed. I began to feel I was no longer the right person for the job. I found myself frustrated and unsatisfied. It seemed unthinkable that I would leave a company I had created, yet I was increasingly unhappy. Then a catalyst occurred that began to move me into a new direction: I was diagnosed with an immune-related illness that was potentially serious. Reducing stress was critical to my living a long and healthy life. I faced my own self-limiting beliefs and fears. I needed to leave the firm, and my role as president, to find the space to reconnect and take care of myself. My sister's children were now grown and more independent. I was able to take more risks. I took my own coaching advice and began an internal journey, and at age forty-eight, I began my first sabbatical. I had just purchased my first home, so I had a place to rest and recuperate. My lifestyle required a steady income, so I negotiated a buyout that gave me a year.

First I did all of the things that I had longed to do over the last ten years that I never had time for. I spent leisurely time alone and with my family. I visited friends I had neglected. I traveled a lot, which opened me up to new possibilities. Everything I did stimulated ideas, and I matched those against the backdrop of what I knew about myself. I found a new inner peace that was, however, mixed with the anxieties and pressures of the unknown.

I began reading and attending conferences on emotional intelligence. I thought about how I could incorporate these new ideas into my work as an executive coach and team facilitator. I also did other fun things I had always wanted to do, like learning to play the Conga drums. As time passed, the ideas for using all of these new elements in my work came together. I designed Team Beat, a team-building facilitation technique, using drumming and rhythm as a metaphor for teams working in sync. Little by little, a new direction began to emerge for the consulting practice I would build.

I was surprised at how long the process took. I wanted answers quickly. I wanted a plan. I wanted to take action. After one year, I still felt that I had more work to do on self-reflection. I realized that I would carry this continued self-analysis and learning with me, probably for the rest of my life. I learned that I had changed over the past ten years, and I got to know my new self better. As I emerged from uncertainty and began to understand what I had and what I wanted to become, I felt more alive and connected to myself, and certainly more healthy.

Now I'm doing what I want, where I want, and how I want. I rebuilt my expertise in corporate coaching and team building, integrating new techniques and ideas I developed during my time off. I have my own practice and can manage my work/life balance more successfully. My work is incredibly rewarding, and my clients are diverse. I've maintained a good relationship with my former partner and company, so I haven't had to lose what I built there.

My work is focused on coaching senior executives. I design and facilitate team processes and events, very often using music. I'm growing every day. I make a point of surrounding myself with supportive friends and family to keep me on track with this new way of living. Without my sabbatical, and the time and space it provided, I would not be where I am today.

| ABOUT THE AUTHORS |

THE SABBATICAL SISTERS are four successful senior executives with careers in diverse fields. When they met, they discovered that they were all sabbatical veterans, joining thousands of men and women who have taken time out from their careers to reflect and renew. The four started calling that a Reboot Break and dubbed themselves the Sabbatical Sisters. Because they found it so important to their own professional careers and personal lives, they wanted to share the concept of "rebooting your life" with others, so they decided to write a book. They talked to over 200 people who have taken time off and researched well over fifty firms that help their employees take sabbaticals in some way. In 2009, they began holding retreats to help people plan and create support systems for taking a sabbatical. Their mission is to help others give themselves the "gift of time." For more information, see their website, *www.rebootbreak.com*, and find them on Facebook, Twitter, and LinkedIn.

CATHERINE ALLEN is a co-author of *The Artist's Way at Work* (William Morrow) with Julia Cameron and Mark Bryan and *Smart Cards: Seizing Strategic Opportunities* (McGraw-Hill Inc) with William Barr. She is known as an innovator and expert in financial services and technology. Her career includes executive positions at Dun & Bradstreet and Citibank, and assistant professorships at several universities. Most recently, she was the founding CEO of BITS, the industry consortium made up of the CEOs of 100 of the largest financial services institutions. Today she owns and manages The Santa Fe Group, a strategic consulting firm of financial industry and technology experts. She sits on the boards of Stewart Title Guaranty, El Paso Electric Company, and Citibank Global Transaction Services, plus the boards of two foundations, the Los Alamos National Laboratory and Museum of New Mexico, and several non-profits. Recently, she was appointed by Governor Bill Richardson to the New Mexico State Investment Council. Catherine has taken two Reboot Breaks. She lives in Santa Fe, New Mexico.

NANCY BEARG has had a forty-year career in international security policy. Her early career was in government at the Department of Defense, National Security Council (White House), Senate Armed Services Committee, and Congressional Budget Office. She was the National Security Advisor to then–Vice President George H.W. Bush and later served on the National Security Council staff when he was president. After one of her Reboot Breaks, Nancy changed gears and moved into the not-for-profit world, directing the International Peace, Security and Prosperity program for the Aspen Institute and then as President and CEO of EnterpriseWorks/VITA, an international development organization. Today Nancy works in the area of conflict prevention and post-conflict peacebuilding, consults on national security, and teaches a university course on leadership. She published five books on national security while at the Aspen Institute. Nancy has taken five Reboot Breaks. She lives in Washington DC.

RITA FOLEY is a corporate director, retired Fortune 500 Global President, and a committed leader in numerous organizations dedicated to improving the health and lives of individuals. Rita sits on the boards of the publicly traded PetSmart and Dresser-Rand, plus two not-for-profit boards: Pro Mujer, a not-for-profit microfinance and health organization operating in Latin America, and The HealthCare Chaplaincy, a leader in palliative care. Rita is an advisor with Crenshaw Associates, leading their board services practice. These appointments follow a very successful business career, which culminated at

MeadWestvaco as Global President of the $1.1B Consumer Packaging Group. Prior to that, Rita held various leadership positions at QAD, Digital Equipment Corp, and Harris Lanier. Rita began her career at Polaroid in St. Albans, England. She has taken four Reboot Breaks. She lives in Brooklyn, NY.

JAYE SMITH is the resident expert on the topic of navigating careers, with more than twenty-five years of experience in the field. Jaye is co-author of *Venus Unbound*(Simon & Schuster, Inc.), a guide for building balance in women . Jaye took a Reboot Break after being the President of Partners in Human Resources International, a consulting firm she co-founded. Today, Jaye continues to work closely with her former firm and is also CEO of her own firm, Breakwater Consulting, where she coaches executives on renewal and leadership as well as designs and facilitates team and organizational effectiveness programs for corporations, not-for-profits, and universities. She is an honored adjunct faculty member at New York University's Center for Career Planning and on the board of Harlem Dowling Westside Center, a foster care and adoption agency. She lives in New York City.

Left to right: Jaye Smith, Catherine Allen, Nancy Bearg, Rita Foley

CPSIA information can be obtained
at www.ICGtesting.com
Printed in the USA
LVOW10s1106300518
578593LV00009B/1/P